PRAISE FOR *MASTER THIEVES*

"A gripping, revelatory book. *Master Thieves* is not only a thrilling heist story but a feat of investigative reporting. The kind of book you can only write if you've lived with a story for twenty years."
—Mitchell Zuckoff, author of *13 Hours* and *Frozen in Time*

"In *Master Thieves*, master reporter Stephen Kurkjian tackles one of the world's greatest unsolved mysteries—the 1990 Gardner Museum art heist in Boston—and leaves the reader feeling like he's cracked the case. This book has the grit and intelligence of a lifelong gangster and the high tension of a midnight caper."
—Ben Bradlee Jr., author of *The Kid: The Immortal Life of Ted Williams*

"Steve Kurkjian is the best reporter in America."
—Dick Lehr, coauthor of *Black Mass*

"Whodunits are irresistible, partly because readers can't wait to find out whether the theories they develop along the way jibe with the ultimate conclusion. Through that lens, *Master Thieves* doesn't deliver; the 'who' remains tantalizingly unclear. But that's OK, and even heightens the sense of criminal mastery." —*Minneapolis Star-Tribune*

"Compelling. . . . It is a journey that takes [Kurkjian] deep into the world of the Mafia and a cast of characters so colourful they could have come from a Martin Scorsese screenplay." —*The Telegraph* (UK)

"If you want to go looking for the lost Gardner horde (and collect the $5-million reward the gallery offers for its return), there's no better place to start than the pages of *Master Thieves*. The museum (and the FBI) could use the help." —*Winnipeg Free Press*

MASTER THIEVES

MASTER THIEVES

**The Boston Gangsters
Who Pulled Off the
World's Greatest Art Heist**

Stephen Kurkjian

PUBLICAFFAIRS
New York

The Library of Congress has cataloged the original edition as follows:

Kurkjian, Stephen A.
    Master thieves : the Boston gangsters who pulled off the world's greatest art heist / Stephen Kurkjian.
        pages   cm
    Includes bibliographical references and index.
    ISBN 978-1-61039-423-9 (hardcover)—ISBN 978-1-61039-424-6 (e-book) 1. Art thefts—Massachusetts—Boston. 2. Theft from museums—Massachusetts—Boston. 3. Isabella Stewart Gardner Museum. I. Title.
N8795.3.U6K87 2015
364.16'287599492—dc23

                                                            2014046852

ISBN: 978-1-61039-632-5 (paperback)

LSC-C
10 9 8 7 6 5 4 3 2

This book is dedicated to my late parents
Anoosh and Rosella Kurkjian, and my aunt Isabelle
Gureghian Totovian, who taught me about life's
greatest gifts—baseball, good writing, and children

CONTENTS

CONTENTS

CAST OF CHARACTERS

RICHARD ABATH. The night watchman who made the grievous errors of allowing the two men dressed as police officers into the museum and then stepping away from the museum's only panic alarm on a ruse by the two thieves.

ANTHONY AMORE. Security director for the museum since 2005 who has worked diligently with the FBI and US attorney's office on the Gardner investigation.

EARLE BERGHMAN. Close friend in Maine of the late mobster Robert Guarente, who believed that Guarente had possession of some of the stolen Gardner paintings. After Guarente's death he introduced Guarente's daughter to a Boston lawyer in the hope of working out a deal to facilitate the recovery of the artwork.

JAMES "WHITEY" BULGER. Notorious Boston mobster whose associates contend sought out who was responsible for the Gardner theft to extract tribute from them for having pulled off such a theft on his turf.

MYLES CONNOR JR. Legendary Boston art thief who contends that he cased the Gardner for a heist with Robert Donati after the pair pulled off the theft of paintings by Andrew Wyeth and his father, N. C. Wyeth, from the Woolworth Estate in Monmouth, Maine, in May 1974.

RICHARD DESLAURIERS. Head of the FBI's Boston office from 2010 to 2013, who announced on the theft's twenty-third anniversary that his agents had determined who was responsible for the theft but said the public's help was still needed to gain the artwork's recovery.

RICHARD DEVLIN. Soldier in the Rossetti gang of East Boston who became an enforcer for Frank Salemme. Killed in a 1994 shootout with members of the rival gang fighting for control of the Boston underworld. Louis Royce, who had cased the Gardner Museum for robbery, says he told Devlin of the museum's poor security and together they operated a cherrypicker to check the museum's windows one night in 1982, only to find they were locked.

ROBERT DONATI. Confidante of and driver for Boston mob leader Vincent Ferrara who reportedly told Ferrara that he had pulled off the Gardner robbery to try to gain Ferrara's release from prison. Donati was brutally beaten to death in September 1991, possibly a victim of the Boston gang war raging at the time.

JOHN DURHAM. Assistant US attorney who spearheaded the prosecution on minor drug charges against Robert Gentile, the low-level criminal believed to be tied to hiding one or more of the stolen paintings at his home in Manchester, Connecticut.

VINCENT "VINNIE" FERRARA. Co-leader of the renegade Boston mob group that fought Frank Salemme for control of the region's underworld in the 1980s and '90s. Ferrara was released from prison in 2005 after serving sixteen years for racketeering when a federal judge found that prosecutors had withheld evidence clearing Ferrara from involvement in the murder of an underling.

ROBERT GENTILE. Low-level crime associate from Manchester, Connecticut, who was convicted of selling prescription drugs to an undercover federal informant, a case he and his lawyer contend was pursued against him to force cooperation on his knowledge of the

Gardner theft. Most incriminating evidence found in a sweep of his house, backyard, and false-bottomed shed was a list showing what the artwork would bring on the black market. Gentile acknowledges that he worked as a cook and security guard for Robert Guarente and Robert Luisi while they were running a cocaine trafficking ring in late 1990s in Boston, and on several occasions drove Luisi to Philadelphia, where Luisi met with mob leaders.

LYLE GRINDLE. Security director of the Gardner Museum at the time of the theft. Knew that the museum lacked several key security components, including a secured control room and a more sophisticated alarm system, but was unable to convince the museum's trustees to raise the funds needed for immediate improvements.

BERNARD GROSSBERG. Boston lawyer who signed a deal with Robert Guarente's daughter and best friend to share reward money if they could prove they could gain recovery of one or more of the paintings. Paint chips given to him by the daughter and friend turned out to be phony.

ELENE GUARENTE. Former wife of the mobster Robert Guarente who told the FBI and Anthony Amore in 2010 that her late husband had given one or more of the stolen paintings to Robert Gentile, his longtime friend from Connecticut.

ROBERT "BOBBY" GUARENTE. The key swingman in the FBI's account of what happened to the stolen paintings after their theft, and a loyalist to Frank Salemme and his underworld gang. The FBI believes Guarente had given some of the artwork, stolen by associates of the Rossetti gang of East Boston or others associated with Carmello Merlino of Dorchester, to Robert Gentile.

ANNE HAWLEY. Appointed director of the museum in 1989, she had been on the job for just six months when the theft occurred. Has spurred FBI investigators, public officials, corporate leaders, even the

Vatican to help in recovery efforts. Led the drive to raise more than $100 million to build a new wing, which opened in 2012 adjacent to the museum.

ARNOLD HIATT. Now-emeritus trustee of the Gardner Museum, was instrumental in having Hawley named as director and has worked hard to maintain the search for the stolen artwork as a priority among investigators.

DAVID HOUGHTON. Small-time hood from Malden, Massachusetts, who allegedly visited Myles Connor in prison in California to say that he and Robert Donati had pulled off the Gardner robbery. Houghton's size, more than three hundred pounds, was far larger than the description of the two thieves, however.

GEOFFREY KELLY. FBI agent in charge of the investigation. Quoted in 2010 as saying there had never been a "concrete sighting" of any of the stolen artwork, but told a Fox TV reporter without providing any details in 2014 that there had been a "confirmed sighting" of one of the paintings.

MARTIN LEPPO. Legendary criminal lawyer who has represented most defendants whose names have been mentioned as having possible ties to the paintings. Convinced prosecutors to combine federal and state prison sentences on Myles Connor in the 1970s after Connor arranged for the return of a Rembrandt stolen from Boston's Museum of Fine Arts, a deal that stirred belief among criminal types that law enforcement will give legal breaks in exchange for return of stolen art.

ROBERT LUISI JR. Boston mobster who operated a wide-scale cocaine trafficking network in 1998–1999 with Robert Guarente in suburban Boston. Reneged on a deal with federal prosecutors to testify against Philadelphia mob associates and accepted a ten-year prison sentence instead. Is now reportedly in the witness protection program.

TOM MASHBERG. Reporter who was taken to a Brooklyn warehouse in 1997 by low-level hood William Youngworth to be shown a purported Rembrandt seascape. Subsequently authored the sensational *Boston Herald* article "We've Seen It" after the viewing. Investigators later questioned whether the heavily varnished seascape could have been unfurled in the way that Mashberg described and contended what Mashberg had seen was not the actual painting but a replica.

A. RYAN MCGUIGAN. Hartford criminal defense lawyer who earned Robert Gentile a reduced prison sentence from the one sought by federal prosecutors. Although he has contended that Gentile has no connection to the Gardner paintings, his law firm signed a deal with Gentile to gain 40 percent of any reward money Gentile might receive if he did arrange for the return of any of the stolen works.

CARMELLO MERLINO. Owner of a Dorchester auto repair garage that served as a center of criminal operations for drug trafficking, fencing stolen material, and plotting to rob an armored car headquarters. Died in prison after the FBI busted up the armored car scheme. Talked much with associates like Robert Guarente and David Turner about arranging the return of the Gardner paintings in the late 1990s. The FBI continues to believe Merlino had a role in the Gardner saga.

CARMEN ORTIZ. US attorney for Massachusetts since 2009. Like several of her predecessors, has pledged immunity from prosecution to whoever can facilitate the return of the artwork stolen from the Gardner Museum.

CHARLES PAPPAS JR. High school chum and criminal partner of David Turner who was shot to death in 1993 after agreeing to testify against Turner in the prosecution related to a Canton, Massachusetts, home invasion. While he snitched on Turner to the state police as being involved in several other crimes, Pappas never alleged that Turner had participated in the Gardner theft, as the FBI believes.

RAYMOND S. PATRIARCA. Head of New England organized crime from 1950 until his death by heart attack in 1984. Ruled with an iron fist, even allegedly ordering that his brother be murdered for failing to detect that federal agents had placed an electronic surveillance device in Patriarca's Providence, Rhode Island, office. His son who succeeded him was unable to bring about peace between the two gangs that fought for control of criminal operations in Boston.

JUREK "ROCKY" ROKOSZYNSKI. Hired by Gardner director Anne Hawley in 2005 to assist in the investigation after his success in recovering two Turner masterpieces for the Tate Gallery in London. Spent much of his time on the Gardner payroll making more than $150,000 chasing down what turned out to be a dead end in Florida.

RALPH ROSSETTI. The head of an East Boston criminal gang loyal to Frank Salemme, who, according to the FBI, had cased the Gardner Museum for robbery in the early 1980s with master thief Louis Royce.

STEPHEN "STEVIE" ROSSETTI. Nephew of Ralph Rossetti who told another associate that he knew the Gardner was vulnerable to being robbed but had passed on the score. Was arrested along with Carmello Merlino and David Turner in 1999 for conspiring to rob an armored car headquarters and is now serving a forty-four-year prison sentence.

LOUIS ROYCE. South Boston native who left his home as a youth and found a warm place to sleep by sneaking into the Gardner Museum before closing time. Turned into one of Boston's most colorful thieves and passed on to associates in the Rossetti gang his deep knowledge of the Gardner facility and the vulnerabilities of the museum's security system.

FRANK "CADILLAC FRANK" SALEMME. Head of a criminal gang in Boston who believed he was entitled to succeed Gennaro (Gerry) Angiulo and his brothers as head of the Boston underworld, but had to fight a renegade group for that control in the 1980s and '90s.

MICHAEL SULLIVAN. US attorney for Massachusetts between 2001 and 2008. Stephen "The Rifleman" Flemmi told him that his boss, James "Whitey" Bulger, had tasked him with finding out who had pulled off the Gardner robbery, but that his efforts were in vain.

DAVID A. TURNER. Braintree High School graduate who was introduced to the thug life after his father's death via various mob activities, including alleged cocaine trafficking, by Robert Guarente in the 1980s. Although he was allegedly in Florida at the time of the heist, rumors continue to swirl about his believed involvement. Turner denied his good friend's statement that he was writing a book that would detail his role in the theft and being set up by the FBI to participate in a scheme to rob an armored car headquarters to force him to tell what he knew of the heist.

WILLIAM YOUNGWORTH. Antiques dealer and low-level member of the Rossetti gang who arranged for *Boston Herald* reporter Tom Mashberg to view what was reported to be the stolen 1633 Rembrandt painting *Storm on the Sea of Galilee* in a Brooklyn warehouse during the early morning hours following a clandestine road trip in August 1997. The FBI and museum officials later rejected that Youngworth had access to the stolen artwork, as he had claimed, when paint chips he had turned over proved to be from another painting of that period but not the famed Rembrandt seascape.

The two best known and most valuable paintings of the thirteen works stolen from the Gardner Museum: Rembrandt's *Storm on the Sea of Galilee* and Vermeer's *The Concert. Courtesy of the Isabella Stewart Gardner Museum.*

INTRODUCTION

ON MARCH 18, 1990, the city of Boston—and the world—
suffered a profound loss when two men dressed as police
officers commandeered the Isabella Stewart Gardner Museum
and pulled off the greatest art theft in world history. Twenty-
five years later the artwork remains missing, and the empty
frames and unfilled spaces on antique desks at the museum
still stand as grim reminders of the poor security and futile
investigative work that followed the theft.

My work initially drew me to the case. As an investigative
journalist for the *Boston Globe* I was a founding member of a
reporting team that exposed massive corruption in the city
of Somerville, Massachusetts, uncovered the unholy alliance
the FBI had formed with notorious gangster James "Whitey"
Bulger, and blew apart the clergy sex abuse scandal inside
the Boston Archdiocese. My reporting had even helped solve
two art thefts. The Gardner Museum heist, I felt, remained as
Boston's last, best secret, and deserved all the reporting skills
I could bring to it.

I was born and raised in Boston, and the Latin School,
which I attended, is located practically across the street from
the fabled museum. My father, an artist himself, was in awe of
the Old Masters whose works graced the Gardner's galleries.

And two of my cousins, both classical pianists, often performed at the Sunday concerts inside the museum's Tapestry Room. I felt so at home at the Gardner that I immediately bonded with an informant—a mobster—over our mutual love of the museum. That connection eventually led to a major break in my investigation.

For a time the leading theory had been that notorious Boston mobster James (Whitey) Bulger had engineered the theft. But then he was caught, after sixteen years on the run, and never once mentioned the paintings in any attempted bargains before his 2013 trial or after his conviction. As for the notion that there was a "Doctor No" figure who had commissioned the heist to get his hands on a favored painting, one need only consider the crime scene. The paintings were carelessly cut from their ancient frames, their windowed fronts shattered, leaving shards of glass throughout the two galleries the robbers pillaged. This was not a surgical strike. This book will hopefully put to rest some of the popular theories about the case—while opening up new leads that point the way to a suspect many have dismissed. . . .

After years of digging that included access to the museum's own files on the case, I came to understand that the answer to the secret of the Gardner heist lay in Boston's own backyard and in its recent history in the war between the two major criminal gangs that had emerged there in the mid-1980s. On one side was the gang led by Frank "Cadillac Frank" Salemme and the other by best friends Vincent "Vinnie" Ferrara and J. R. Russo. They fought for dominance for nearly a decade, battling over every criminal score imaginable: armored car and bank heists, bookmaking, and prostitution, and most remarkably, as I discovered, the masterpieces inside the Isabella Stewart Gardner Museum.

In a March 2013 press conference that led to national attention, the FBI sketched out in the vaguest of terms a scenario that pointed to the involvement of a criminal network stretching from Boston to Maine to Hartford that it believed was behind the theft and stashing of the paintings. Although no suspects were named that day, this book will show in compelling detail the FBI's theory of this crime—and a number of holes in it.

For one, though the FBI focused on identifying who was responsible for the crime, to me, the secret to determining what had happened to the stolen masterpieces required figuring out not only who was responsible but also why they did it. Why would anyone seek to carry out a robbery on the scale of the Gardner heist, only to keep the paintings in secret for more than two decades? Why, after a young thief named Louis Royce realized in 1981 that the Gardner Museum was vulnerable to theft, did it take nine years for someone to actually rob it? After years of investigating this case, these questions continued to nag at me.

To answer them, I have had to take a deep dive into the inner workings of Boston's notorious underworld and gained the trust of some of its most flamboyant and pivotal figures. They ushered me into a world previously unknown to most people. In many ways, the trail I followed in the Gardner case was uniquely Boston, a historic but small city where bank robber and bank president can live side by side in the same neighborhood, or, as with the infamous Bulger family, where the notorious gang leader and State Senate president were brothers.

So no one blinked when I passed on to the FBI the lead that a Massachusetts State Police captain had uncovered that a Gardner Museum gallery guard had cashed one of his monthly retirement checks at an after-hours club owned by another mobster and frequented by several whose names had been mentioned as possible suspects in the case. Whether it was followed up or not depended on the judgment of the sole agent on the case.

This book also delves deep into the investigation of the Gardner case and how it was beset by carelessly blown leads and missed opportunities, raising the question of whether it was most effective for the FBI to be solely responsible for leading it.

Although the individual agents assigned to the case have worked diligently to chase down even the most ridiculous lead, the organization has failed to penetrate the netherworld of Boston's criminal gangs in pursuit of a recovery. And unlike investigations in similar cases in Europe, where teams of investigators work tirelessly and with the full backing of their governments and the art-loving citizens of their countries, the Gardner case has been relegated to as low a priority as the FBI can perhaps afford it.

Anne Hawley, the director of the Gardner Museum since before the theft, is among the most frustrated by the investigation's lack of success. In its aftermath, Hawley used every contact and resource available to her, from US senators to the Vatican, to prod the investigation and convince the public of the extent the loss of these masterpieces represented. That she has been virtually alone in these appeals marks the difference in how the Gardner theft has been viewed in America.

The heist deserves to be treated like a national loss, drawing the same priority and availability of sophisticated resources that responded to the Boston Marathon bombing, and helped spur the city's recovery from that tragedy.

Until that happens, the continued absence of those masterpieces from the Gardner's galleries will deny newcomers and devotees to the art world, whether world traveler or neighborhood resident, the beauty and sophistication that was such a major part of Boston's contribution to the civilized world.

PART I
THE HEIST

CHAPTER ONE

ROYCE

JUST MONTHS AFTER BEING PAROLED from Massachusetts state prison, where he had recently finished serving a seventeen-year sentence for kidnapping and attempted extortion, Louis Royce, now well into his seventies, walks easily through the Isabella Stewart Gardner Museum. Measured by his rough appearance and rougher past, he seems an unlikely person to be strolling through the galleries of one of Boston's most cultured sites. Considering Royce has spent most of his adult life in federal and state prisons, you'd think he'd be out of place standing alongside the refined blue bloods and mon-eyed tourists who customarily make their way through the Gardner. But, walking beside him, I sense a remarkable ease.

It's been nearly thirty years since Royce has been inside the museum, but he ambles through the rooms—albeit with a slight limp from that long-ago bullet wound—like someone who knows every inch of every gallery and staircase if not every painting on the Gardner's walls. And he does.

The Raphael Room, on the second floor of the four-story building, is ornate but tasteful.

Its parquet floors, high ceiling, and deep red walls make it feel—like the rest of the museum—like a home rather than an art museum. As we stop at one of the floor-to-ceiling windows that overlook Boston's Fens neighborhood, Royce brushes the top of an antique desk and a smile creases his well-worn face.

"This is it," he says, pointing to the painting encased in a gold frame that leans on the desk. "This is what I wanted to take."

The painting, Raphael's *Lamentation Over the Dead Christ*, painted in 1504 and part of the Gardner collection since 1900, is a stunning piece. It isn't large, but the details and the pathos it evokes are palpable. Just to hear Royce speak the thought of stealing such an exquisite piece in such an artistically sacred place is disturbing. But as I look into his eyes, I know he is dead serious.

LOUIS F. ROYCE was only thirteen years old when he began visiting—and staying overnight, hidden away—at the Isabella Stewart Gardner Museum. Intended as a benevolent gift by a millionairess to the people of Boston in honor of her late industrialist husband, the museum has represented the best of what the city stands for since it opened its doors in 1903. And no one has taken advantage of that gift quite like Louis Royce.

As a kid, Royce grew up hardscrabble in the tough, crime-ridden neighborhoods of South Boston. But something about the Gardner spoke to him and on his second visit, among some of the world's most expensive paintings and antiques, Royce found a comfortable and well-hidden spot in a third-floor gallery and spent the night.

His first visit had been a few months before, with his eighth-grade classmates from the Patrick Gavin Junior High School in South Boston. The field trip was intended to show the kids from one of Boston's poorest neighborhoods some of the city's finer things: beautiful paintings, antiques, and tapestries. But it wasn't the artwork that Royce remembered most about the museum when he ran away from his South Boston home a short time later. His fond memories of the artwork would come decades later, after he had become one of Boston's most successful thieves, and he saw the museum and its decrepit security system as the score of a lifetime. No, what the youthful Royce remembered most from that school field trip in 1950 was how warm the Gardner had been. So Royce sought the comfort of the museum after he ran away.

After a day spent in petty crime, running numbers and bets for established bookies in downtown Boston, and shoplifting out of department and grocery stores, Royce made his way back to the Fenway neighborhood and walked into the museum before its late-afternoon closing. He made his way to the third floor, and the long narrow gallery that runs along the building's eastern side. There he squeezed himself under the ornate antique table with a heavy crimson tapestry hanging over its edge, giving him the perfect hiding place. Under the table, below the painted terra-cotta of Matteo Civitali's fifteenth-century *Virgin Adoring the Child*, Louis Royce found a new home and fell asleep.

What had driven young Royce to run away, and ultimately into the life of crime that led to the plan to rob the Gardner Museum, was learning a family secret so devastating that he remembered it vividly when he recalled it for me sixty years later.

"The man I thought was my father wasn't," he said.

Although his parents were poor, with seven kids and two adults jammed into a three-bedroom, cold-water flat a block away from a busy subway station, a bond was shared among the family. The kids checked one another's homework before going to bed at night, and any extra money that any one of them earned was always split with the others. Louis, being the oldest, followed that rule to the letter. Every week he turned over the few dollars he'd earned as a newspaper delivery boy to his mother, who let him keep for himself the few tips that he made.

It was a threadbare existence, but Royce remembers those early boyhood years with fondness. That is, until the day his mother sent him downtown to Boston's City Hall to get a copy of his birth certificate so he could get his license to shine shoes. It was time he earned some real money after school, not just the pennies he made delivering the papers.

"People like you, your teachers like you, the priests like you. You'd be good at shining shoes," his mother, Lulu, told him.

It was on that trip to City Hall that Louis Royce found out the secret his mother had been keeping from him his whole young life. John E. Royce, the man young Louis had known for as long as he could remember, who had tucked him in at night and even whipped him when he'd gotten caught in a lie or another transgression, was not in fact his father. Indeed, the space on the birth certificate Louis picked up at City Hall that day was blank where it listed "name of father."

When Louis returned home that afternoon, he confronted his mother: "Why isn't Dad's name on my birth certificate?" At the kitchen table, before the other kids got home from school, Lulu told her son the truth.

He had been born Louis Morrill, having been given his mother's maiden name as his last name. Before she married John Royce, Lulu told him, she had been involved with a married Gloucester fisherman and had two children with him: a daughter, who was born with Down syndrome and had lived her life in a state institution, and Louis.

Although a year after Louis found the birth certificate John Royce would sign the papers to adopt him, it was too late.

"I felt empty," he recalled to me, sixty years later. "All of a sudden I was somehow different from the brothers and sisters I'd grown up with. I didn't belong."

After his mother broke the news to him, Royce headed to his bedroom to stuff the few clothes he owned into a paper bag. Then his younger brother Billy walked in.

"I heard," Billy said, flopping onto the bottom tier of the two bunk beds squeezed into the bedroom. "Ma told me."

Louis said nothing and, not wanting to show he had been crying, didn't even look at his younger brother.

"Where are you going to go?" Billy asked. "You know, you don't have to go nowhere. You can still live here with us like nothing happened. You didn't do anything wrong."

"I know I didn't do anything wrong," Louis shot back, the rage boiling up inside him. "This isn't my fault; it's theirs," he said, nodding to the kitchen, where his mother was getting dinner ready. "But it explains a lot."

Before Billy could say anything, Louis reminded him about his last birthday. There had been no cake, no celebration, as there had been for Billy's as well as their sisters'. And instead of walking into the house with a gift, like a football or a baseball glove, their father had handed him an envelope when he got home that day, late and drunk as usual. Inside, without a card, there was a single dollar bill.

"So what?" Billy shrugged. "You can take any of our stuff. You know that."

Louis clenched his hands into fists and walked over to Billy, fully intending to jump him and show him how furious he was. But Louis and Billy both knew that even if he landed a punch, that would be it. There would be no beating. Although Billy was several years younger than Louis, he was already catching up to him in height and size. The crazed toughness that would later manifest itself in his shooting two Massachusetts prison guards, whom Billy thought had frisked his mother too closely when she came to visit him in prison, was already beginning to show up. Though he wasn't even a teenager yet, neighborhood kids knew not to mess with Billy Royce. He was stronger and tougher, and, as Louis had learned for sure earlier in the day, Billy had in him something Louis did not: their father's DNA.

When he left the Royce house that night, Louis became a "boy of the streets," skipping school whenever he felt like it, hanging out in Scollay Square, Boston's seediest area, a mecca of strip joints, all-night movie houses, bars, and diners.

"The way I felt, that man wasn't my father," Royce told me, thinking back. "There was no reason for me to stay in that house."

When he recounted the story to me, all those years later, it was clear that just thinking about it again made Louis ashamed and embarrassed. Soon that sense of being an outsider, of never belonging, became a strong part of his psychology. He compensated by being loyal to the cohorts he spent his life in crime with, especially the members of the East Boston gang he joined in the mid-1970s after walking away from a minimum-security facility in Boston's Mattapan neighborhood. He was always doing favors for them, it seemed: turning over the details of armored cars and banks he'd cased and figured were vulnerable to being robbed or accepting culpability for a crime so another gang member might evade prosecution. Or turning in stolen artwork so the gang leader might stay out of jail.

The urge to be part of a group, no matter a criminal gang or a cell-block group of prisoners, defined Louis Royce, and regardless of whether the enterprise was legal, it meant that Royce never—absolutely never—informed on anyone.

But first Louis had to learn the lesson of what loyalty could bring on the streets of Scollay Square. Right away, Royce loved the life he found there. He felt at home in the seedy Boston district populated by burlesque halls and rough bars, that attracted gamblers, thrill seekers, and down-and-outers. He quickly began running numbers for bookies like the infamous Ilario Zannino (aka Larry Baione), who rose to become one of Boston's biggest organized crime figures.

And Royce, and his inimitable abilities as a thief, were remembered by them. When Zannino was being prosecuted for bookmaking at a local district court, Royce and an associate broke into the courthouse during a weekend night in 1970, picked the lock on the evidence safe, and stole the cash and other incriminating records seized in Zannino's arrest. Although Royce was prosecuted after police arrested him and found in his wallet some of the marked bills he had taken from the safe, he recalls with pride that Zannino paid him $10,000 for the job, which resulted in the charges against Zannino being dropped. More important, Royce earned trust and respect within Boston's crime world by refusing to cooperate with the police who arrested him.

"I figured this was the family that I had now, so no matter what scrapes we got in, I'd keep my mouth shut," said Royce.

His vulnerability, his need to make friends and gain respect, made Royce an oddity in the underworld. It also explained his loyalty to some gang members and not to others. In fact, except for being a master thief, Royce had few personal vices. He didn't smoke, drink, or do drugs. And while it may have caused some smart-ass comments among his criminal associates, he made no secret of his being gay.

No doubt, though, there was a threatening side to Royce. He was certainly willing to introduce violence to gain the upper hand. But even better, he liked people to know that his brother Billy was a criminal with a wild, violent streak. And

Louis F. Royce, circa 1981, considered by the FBI to be one of Boston's most artful thieves, cased the museum for a heist, having known about its poor security since sleeping in its galleries as a runaway youth.

while Louis Royce had committed dozens of robberies, two of his three longest sentences were for violent crimes. In fact, when he was planning the Gardner Museum heist, Royce was an escapee from federal detention for an elaborate kidnapping and extortion plan he'd been nabbed for ten years earlier.

In the early 1970s, Royce and several accomplices had forced their way into the home of a banker and his family in Lincoln, Rhode Island. While the family was held hostage, Royce drove the husband to his bank and, before it opened for business, stole more than $100,000 in cash from its safe. The crime came undone when Royce was arrested after he checked himself into a Boston hotel using his mother's maiden name—Morrill—to sign the register. He was unaware that Boston police had just commenced one of their biggest manhunts ever in search of a criminal named William Morrill Gilday, who was on the run after killing a police officer during a local bank holdup.

But easily his biggest heist, and a measure of how daring Royce could be, came in December 1981, when he arranged the robbery of a South Shore bank with a close friend, Richard Devlin, who had been released from prison on a furlough just an hour before the heist.

Even though he was ten years older than Devlin, Royce was drawn to the younger man when they served time together in the 1960s at a Massachusetts state prison. The two shared an insatiable interest in criminal mayhem, and balanced each other well. Royce liked to plan his heists meticulously; Devlin delighted in carrying them out.

"I liked him," Royce told me, remembering those early days fondly. "He was a dynamic guy and if you stayed on his good side, which I made sure I did, he was always talking one score or another."

Although he would be released from prison the following month, Devlin went ahead and participated in the Rockland bank robbery while he was on a daylong furlough from a minimum-security facility in Plymouth, Massachusetts. During his first term as governor of Massachusetts, Michael S. Dukakis had broadened the state's prison furlough program in an effort to ease the re-entry of prisoners into society.

Despite the program's good intentions, there was little oversight, which led to numerous examples of prisoners committing petty crimes while on work release. Most famously, Willie Horton, a convicted murderer, never returned from a weekend furlough and two years later was arrested for raping a woman and assaulting her fiancé in Maryland. The case came to light during Dukakis's 1988 presidential campaign and proved his political undoing.

Devlin, too, exploited the furlough program to continue his life in crime. On Saturday, December 19, 1981, Devlin signed himself out of his minimum-security facility at 6:45 A.M., ostensibly to drive to his job nearby. But instead Devlin drove north to a rest area off Route 3 in Marshfield, half an hour away, where Royce was waiting for him along with another member of the Rossetti gang in a van the two had stolen earlier that morning.

With Royce driving Devlin's car and Devlin in the stolen van, the trio drove north another fifteen miles to the South Shore Mall in Hanover, and the Rockland Trust Company.

"I'd scoped out the bank weeks in advance," Royce says now with the pride only a master thief could muster. "I knew every in and out of the place. When we got there we could see the folks inside counting out the cash. They were preparing for the arrival of the armored car, which always came right when the bank opened, at 9 A.M."

So a half hour before the truck's arrival, the thieves parked their stolen van in the lot of a nearby school and Royce dropped off Devlin and the third man just outside the bank. The men lugged the steel frame of a truck tire out of Royce's trunk and hurled it through the bank's window. Then, brandishing rifles, they jumped through the shattered window and ordered the three petrified tellers to hand over the bags of cash they had been filling.

While the pair were inside the bank, Royce drove back out to nearby Route 3 and parked beneath an overpass. He opened the hood of his car as if it had broken down. There was nothing wrong with the engine, but it allowed Royce to stay put in an accessible place without attracting suspicion. In fact, Royce had outfitted the car with storage areas to stash the rifles that were being used in the robbery along with the money bags from the heist.

Within minutes, before police could respond to the bank's alarms, Devlin and his partner were out of the bank and driving to the top of the overpass, where Devlin jumped out of the stolen van and scampered down with the money and rifles to

Royce's waiting car. While Royce and Devlin got away clean, their associate drove the stolen van to the parking lot of the nearby Norwell High School and abandoned it. Police located it a short time later.

No one was ever arrested in the Rockland Trust theft, but Hanover police who investigated the case told me that Royce's story checked out, down to the very last detail. In the ensuing months in Boston, Royce said, he and Devlin settled into the Rossetti gang and cased several major scores, including breaking into the Gardner Museum.

NEARLY A YEAR BEFORE, on a January night in 1981, Royce walked into Jacques, a typical gay bar in Boston's Bay Village. It was wild and a little bit seedy, with lots of mirrors and glitter and red-cushioned, stationary stools set around a horseshoe-shaped bar. Royce supposed it was meant to be swanky, but the redbrick industrial-style floor was the real giveaway. It was a dump.

In this dive, the seeds of the infamous Gardner Museum heist were sown.

"I know this girl. She's my girlfriend. She says her father is one of the richest men in Boston," a young man at the bar told Royce matter-of-factly.

"Girlfriend?" *What the hell?* Royce thought. He'd been at the bar looking for a little company.

"Bisexual," the kid said flatly. Royce shrugged. A career gangster then in his forties, Royce couldn't be picky. The younger men who typically frequented Jacques accepted him, and maybe even found him attractive. With his thick afro and love of hard rock music, he did what he could to fit in and more often than not he was able to find a desirable twenty-something for a quick encounter or even to take home. What he didn't usually do was mix business with pleasure.

"He's got one of the best houses in Newton," the kid went on.

Royce was getting more interested, and not just in the young man. Rich? Newton? *That's one of the most desirable suburbs outside of Boston*, he thought.

Royce never checked out what the kid was telling him about how he had gotten access to the house and the family, but he was convincing—the house contained expensive jewelry and "an amazing collection of art." After a little more small talk, the kid told Royce that if he was looking for an easy score and was willing to share the proceeds of what was stolen, he might be able to gain him access to the house.

"Tell me about the art," Royce said.

"Mostly it's numbered prints. Chagall. Dalí."

"Wait a minute," Royce interrupted. "Dalí? He's my favorite."

Although he had been breaking into well-to-do homes and condos in Newton and neighboring Brookline for several years, this would be the first time Royce would be stealing art. But he'd always loved art.

Over the next several weeks, the pair concocted a plan. Royce gave his new boyfriend a pad that allowed him to copy the keys to the front door of the Newton home, as well as to the alarm system. The boyfriend had told Royce the family visited Florida every winter, so all they had to do was be patient.

In mid-February Royce met the boy again at Jacques and learned the Newton couple had planned their Florida vacation for the last two weeks of February. Now Royce had to put the final pieces of the puzzle in place.

Days before the theft was to take place, Royce approached Ralph Rossetti and his nephew, Stephen. Hardened criminals, the Rossettis had become like family to Royce. Well, at least

Ralph was. Stevie was too much of a hothead, and too young for Royce's liking.

About a year earlier, a botched robbery attempt had left Royce recuperating from a gunshot wound for over a month, during which time he reached out to Ralph Rossetti for a place in his gang. Royce had always relied on a loose network of friends in crime, but after being shot during one aborted robbery and turned on by a couple of accomplices with whom he had robbed a bank in Dorchester, he decided that the cover provided by being part of a proper crime family would help protect him. The elder Rossetti, having served time in prison with Royce in the 1960s and knowing of his career as an active and aggressive B&E—breaking and entering—artist, welcomed him.

On the night of February 21, 1981, Royce and the Rossettis were ready for the Newton heist and drove together in Royce's late-model Cadillac from East Boston to Newton. As the boyfriend had told him, there was one light on in the living room as if to warn potential robbers that the house was occupied. It was not, and Royce, with his headlights off, pulled into the long driveway and parked.

Royce used the copied keys to disarm the alarm system and to get in through the front door. Once inside, also by design, he broke a downstairs window so it would look like the thieves had gained entrance that way, and that it was not the inside job it really was. The crew took more than $50,000 in jewelry that night, as well as eleven paintings and prints. Based on Mike's information, Royce and the Rossettis knew exactly where everything was, so getting the jewelry was easy. The art took more time.

Once all the artwork had been taken from its wall placements, each piece was placed in a separate bag and brought out and stacked in the trunk of Royce's car.

Now the question was simply where to stash their booty.

"Let's drive this haul over to A-Z, like we agreed," Royce told the Rossettis before they left the Newton house. Royce had bought from a friend a rundown antiques shop, A-Z Trading, in Hyde Park, a blue-collar neighborhood of Boston, and the place had served him well. It was filled floor to ceiling with cheap pieces of furniture, mirrors, and second-hand items, but it also allowed him to hide valuables from other break-ins.

"No way," Stevie Rossetti said. "This is too much stuff for your penny-ante store. Let's get it over to Eastie, then we can figure out what we've got." Rossetti was referring to East Boston, the neighborhood that was home to the Rossetti gang, and a hotbed of mob activity in the early 1980s.

Immediately, Royce knew it had been a mistake for Ralph to bring along his nephew. Royce and the younger Rossetti had been clashing for months, ever since Royce had told Ralph of his plan for robbing an armored car. Stevie had loved the plan when Royce explained it to him and Ralph. But the younger Rossetti balked at the gang Royce had pulled together to handle the robbery. "They're like you, too old," he'd said bluntly, ending the debate over whose people they were going to use. Royce had looked at Ralph, and knew he could never overrule Stevie.

The senior Rossetti, hunched and contemplative, never looked up. "We can always use younger men."

"Never try to overrule my nephew," Rossetti later told Royce ominously. "That's not how we do it here."

The Rossetti gang was growing in reputation on Boston's crime scene. They added members of motorcycle gangs to their numbers and extended their criminal activity beyond armored car and bank robberies to ripping off drug dealers and big-time card games and even hijacking trucks loaded with oriental rugs. When a gang war loomed in Boston in the mid-1980s, the Rossettis quickly threw their support behind

"Cadillac Frank" Salemme and battled against a rival gang that was fighting for control of the Boston underworld.

Royce knew he would never overtake Stevie Rossetti in stature in the gang, so he kept his mouth shut. He drove back to East Boston, wanting to banter about the score they had just pulled off without a hitch. But seeing Stevie was his sullen self, Royce kept quiet as the elder Rossetti gave him directions back to East Boston. There, atop a hill overlooking Suffolk Downs, Boston's only racetrack, they carried the stolen artwork into the basement of Ralph Rossetti's house.

Soon the local press was sniffing around, trumpeting that the theft was one of the largest home break-ins in Newton history and that the thieves appeared to have gained entry to the house by breaking a downstairs window. Two Newton police detectives had been assigned to the case. Royce and the Rossettis laid low, waiting for the news of the theft to disappear from the pages of the Boston newspapers so Royce could see what some of his best black-market fences, whom he'd used in the past to move some of the finer items that passed through the A-Z, might be willing to offer for the artwork.

That was the plan, at least. Unbeknownst to Royce, Stevie Rossetti had decided to do a little freelancing.

On his own, less than three weeks after the theft, Stevie Rossetti visited his uncle's basement and took one of the prints and photographs of several of the other stolen paintings to a connection who had expressed interest in purchasing some of the artwork. Stevie reported back to Ralph Rossetti the next day. "I've got a guy who's interested in buying everything," he told his uncle excitedly.

The first Royce heard about it was when Ralph Rossetti called him. "Stevie's found someone who is interested in doing business," Ralph said.

Although he was upset that the younger Rossetti had reached out to a stranger on his own, Royce agreed to a meeting outside an Italian restaurant near busy Maverick Square in East Boston. He knew he didn't have a choice.

Royce easily warmed to the stranger as they sat in his Cadillac. He talked knowledgeably about Dalí's work, and the value of what had been stolen. But what really won Royce over was when the stranger said he'd heard of Royce's proficiency as a thief from another fence with whom Royce had worked in Providence. The Rossettis, who sat in the backseat, seemed as impressed with the stranger as they were with Royce's growing reputation.

"I'll give you $50,000 for the whole score," he told Royce. "But I need more than these photos. Before I deliver you any money I need proof of what you've got. All of it. Everything."

"I'll tell you what," Royce countered. "I don't know you. You say we have friends? You seem to know what we've got. How do I know you're not FBI?"

Royce paused and threw a handkerchief on the stranger's lap. "Put this around your eyes and I'll take you to the stuff."

Although they were less than five minutes from Rossetti's house, where the artwork was still stashed, Royce went from one side street to another, weaving through East Boston, making sure they weren't being followed. Royce knew the FBI wouldn't let one of their own out of sight with three known mobsters, so, not seeing any tail or obvious surveillance, he soon relaxed and started talking.

When they got to Rossetti's house Royce instructed his passenger to remove his blindfold. By this time he was getting comfortable, and knew that after the blindfolded drive he had the stranger's full attention. "You know, I'm planning another score that might interest you," Royce said. "The artwork there makes this look like small potatoes." Royce handed over a guidebook to the Gardner Museum.

"Me and the old man have a plan," Royce boasted, nodding toward the book. "Anything catch your eye?"

"Are you kidding?" the stranger said with a laugh, flipping through the guidebook. "Let's see what you've got first. Let's see how this goes."

Royce led the group to the backyard, to a door not easily seen from the street. That's when he noticed the stranger's shoes.

"Did you see those shoes? Look at that shine," Royce whispered to the elder Rossetti, who blew off Royce's concerns.

"Let's do this," Ralph said, and the meeting went forward.

They showed the stranger all eleven pieces from the score at the Newton home.

"This is nice, quality stuff," the stranger said. "$50,000 for everything, right? I don't have time to raise that kind of cash. How about $10,000 for the Dalís?"

Three prints for $10k? Royce nodded approvingly to the Rossettis.

A meeting was scheduled, but the stranger kept putting Royce off. Before long Royce gave up on him. "He doesn't have the dough," Royce told Ralph Rossetti.

Then, in late August, six months after their initial meeting, the stranger called Royce.

"Let's make a deal," he said.

As he continued to wait for an opportunity to cash in his big score, Royce finally heard the magic words from his fence.

"Where can we meet?" the stranger asked. "I've got a buyer for the stuff myself, and I want to do this deal as quickly as possible."

"Stevie will meet you late tomorrow afternoon," Royce said. "East Boston. Outside the entrance to the Sumner Tunnel."

The next day, Royce and Ralph Rossetti sat in Royce's car about a block away from the arranged site for the meeting, a tunnel that carries cars to and from downtown Boston and Logan Airport. But before the younger Rossetti even arrived on the scene with three of the Dalí prints, a swarm of FBI agents descended on Royce's car and arrested him and the elder Rossetti. They also seized three of the paintings stolen from the Newton home: one lithograph signed by Chagall and two signed by Dalí.

While Stevie Rossetti was able to elude capture, Royce and Ralph Rossetti were arrested and arraigned on multiple theft charges in Middlesex County Superior Court. They made bail, but Royce returned to court less than a year later to face the charges. He knew he had little recourse but to plead to the break-in at the Newton house. But he had an offer to make to the prosecutors.

"If you drop the charges against Ralph, I'll tell you where you can find the rest of the score," he told prosecutors.

The deal was struck, though nothing was said about it when Royce appeared in court. Less than a month later police announced a raid of a North Shore motel during which they'd recovered the valuable paintings and prints that had been stolen from the Newton home. Neither Royce's nor Rossetti's names were made public as being involved in the paintings' recovery.

I FIRST MET LOUIS ROYCE in a private room at a Massachusetts state prison, in a section where inmates could meet with their friends or lawyers. He was in the final months of the seventeen-year sentence for pleading guilty to masterminding a scheme to kidnap and hold for ransom a well-to-do Boston restaurant owner.

"This is the third long bid I've done since the early '70s," he told me, estimating that he had spent about five years during the past four decades on the street, with two of those years as an escapee from federal custody.

In fact, Royce's criminal record shows that even as a twelve-year-old he was being arrested by Boston police. But those early run-ins with the law, according to his record for being a "stubborn child," soon turned more serious as he became adept at larceny and breaking and entering.

Despite the grimness of his past, Royce was upbeat when we met and I told him that I wanted his help in figuring out the Gardner case. Over the next several months we met more than a dozen times and I came to appreciate how important Royce's experiences were to solving the case. Royce swore he did not know who was responsible for the theft; he had been in prison when it had taken place. But I knew that if I could get him talking, all these years later, he would surely tell me whom he'd told about how vulnerable the museum was to a major theft, not to mention the details of his elaborate plan, and that in turn might help me to determine who pulled it off.

Royce was blunt about his motive. He had two reasons for wanting to see the case solved.

"I figure they still owe me my 15 percent," he said. Under the norms of the criminal life, the person who learns of a potential score, or hatches the plan for it, and passes it on to others, is due 15 percent of the profits of the theft, depending on the tipster's clout with the actual thieves. "As I see it, with the way it works in my world, someone owes me a lot of money."

"You find out who did it," Royce said. "I'll make my case with them."

Also, Royce said, regardless of who had ordered it and why, the specific purpose of the theft way back in 1990 had long since passed. "Maybe they [the paintings] were taken to get someone out of jail, but that obviously hasn't happened. So they're just laying somewhere now, unseen and unappreciated. They should be back with the museum now."

Before I spoke to Royce I knew I had to check to make certain of his bona fides. I needed to be sure he had indeed been a master thief who had studied how to rob the Gardner

Museum and that he was a trusted member of one of Boston's most aggressive underworld gangs and had brought the secret of how to rob the museum into that mob.

Soon I had the testament of the FBI's leading undercover agent in New England during the 1970s and 1980s.

"He was the best thief I'd ever seen," FBI special agent William Butchka told me, without hesitation. "He was clever, and he'd study a job for however long it took to figure out the best way of pulling it off successfully."

As for the possibility that the plan to rob the Gardner Museum had originated with Royce, Butchka said, "I had never heard anyone talking about it before him. The next time I heard about the museum after that, it had just been robbed."

I had been reporting on the Gardner theft for the *Boston Globe* since 1997, and getting Royce to talk seemed a tremendous advantage. Confidential files attested to his having cased the museum for a major robbery and, since this was the first time he had spoken about it, I felt confident he could provide the link that would lead to a breakthrough.

Unlike the FBI, whose strategy for finding the stolen artwork had evolved into a game of waiting for someone to call to make a deal or the Hail Mary of waiting for an anonymous tip, Royce offered a different path. The key to recovering the artwork lay with the crew who had stolen it, and Royce surely knew who they were.

Still, I wondered if it were possible that this eighth-grade dropout, who had spent most of his adult years behind bars, could hold the secret to this infamous case.

WHILE WITH THE ROSSETTI GANG in the early 1980s, Royce says, he made several visits to the Gardner Museum. He had not been back to the museum since his boyhood, but now it was more than a warm place to spend the night. During his ensuing years as a criminal, Royce had hatched a plan to rob the Gardner of some of its most precious artifacts.

Royce told me about a fellow gangster who had taken part in the theft of a valuable Rembrandt from a Worcester museum in the 1970s. Royce had been impressed with the favorable buzz the heist had garnered in the criminal underworld.

Although a guard had been shot in the Worcester robbery, Royce was convinced that the security at the Gardner was so lax that he could pull in a huge score, and best of all, without any violence.

Royce wasn't looking to hit the Gardner to secure the prison release of an associate or strike a plea bargain deal, as had become the custom in the gangland underworld. Instead, he had riches in mind. Royce and his fellow gangsters put the word out, seeking a commission from a wealthy art collector connected to the underworld. Then he made a detailed study of the museum's security system and decided that, while a number of approaches for breaking into the building could be made, the easiest time to hit the museum was at night. The museum held chamber music concerts on Tuesday evenings that were lightly attended and overseen by only one or two guards. With Rossetti in tow, Royce planned to walk into the concerts and ignite several smoke bombs. In the ensuing chaos, they intended to rush to the galleries where the paintings they planned to steal were hanging and make as fast a getaway as they could manage.

Of course, once inside, Royce planned to find a way of getting his hands on the crucifix scene painted by Raphael in 1504, captured in a rich golden frame, *Lamentation Over the Dead Christ*, purchased by Mrs. Gardner in 1900 just as she was moving forward with constructing her museum in Boston's Fens neighborhood.

Royce showed the score to Richard Devlin, who was immediately keen on the plan. Devlin knew from his brother and a former neighborhood accomplice, both of whom had been arrested for trying to fence stolen paintings in Florida in the late '70s, the value of rare masterpieces. He was more than willing to accompany Royce when he scoped out the Gardner.

As fate would have it, one night while driving past a construction site near the museum, the pair noticed several pieces of heavy equipment apparently being used in a renovation job. Who needed police uniforms and smoke bombs when you had a cherry-picker truck left right there for the taking?

In an instant Royce decided this was the simplest way for him to grab the piece he had coveted for so long. He knew the Raphael crucifix scene was right there by the second-floor window, so the two men simply "borrowed" the man-lift.

"This is perfect," Royce thought as he drove the piece of equipment the three miles to the museum. At the corner of the Fens and Palace Road, right in front of the Gardner, the pair made it seem that they were members of an emergency utility crew and set up orange cones around a nearby. . . . With Devlin providing lookout, Royce swung the bucket of the cherry-picker into place, close to the museum's second-floor windows.

"I was within fifteen feet of it, but I could see the damned window was locked," Royce remembers. "I considered breaking the glass, but I knew it would have set off an alarm. And there was no way we'd be able to get away in time with that piece of equipment. I waved off Richie [Devlin], and that was it." Thankfully, keeping the windows locked was one security precaution the museum always maintained.

Although they may not have known about the incident with the cherry-picker, the FBI knew of Royce's interest in robbing the Gardner from their undercover encounter with him and the Rossettis trying to sell the valuable prints they had stolen from the Newton home.

Louis Royce — Aug. 31 —5'8" 180lb 8/27/37 Brown hair Blue eyes
Ralph Rossetti 14 yrs. in jail Armed
Yellow + Blue — most accessible
Could close get Raphael on easel

Tues. in Sept.
Man inside — a guard
Not sure whether it is willing or unwitting
complice.

320 O'Neill blvd. #10
Attleboro, MA.

4 cases pending
Store in Roslindale   A to Z Trading Post
159 Belgrade Avenue

29 Whipple Ave.
Roslindale

Notes taken by the Gardner Museum's deputy director during a confidential meeting with FBI agents on September 23, 1981, held to inform the museum that it was in danger of being robbed by master thief Louis Royce and Ralph Rossetti, head of an East Boston gang.

Within days of recovering the artwork stolen from the Newton residence, the FBI had reached out to officials at the Gardner with a message.

"You're going to be hit."

"Lyle, we've been contacted by the FBI and two agents want to come in to see us," said a 1981 note from Linda Hewitt, the Gardner Museum's deputy director, to Lyle Grindle, its security director.

The next week, on September 23, 1981, FBI special agent Edward Clark and a second agent were ushered into the museum's small first-floor library. Around a small wooden table, they shook hands with the three people who were most responsible for the museum's safety: Grindle; Roland "Bump" Hadley, the museum's director; and Hewitt.

Clark, a textbook example of an FBI agent, trim with sharp features, a crisp suit, and an almost military demeanor, didn't waste any time with pleasantries. Instead he opened the meeting candidly.

"You've got a problem, my friends. Some people have found a hole in your security system."

The Gardner staff, not used to such brusque talk, especially from law enforcement, bristled.

"The FBI's Boston office has come in contact with men who have been working with a gang from East Boston," Clark went on, in a formal, affected FBI manner the staff recognized from television and movies. "They're intent on breaking in and robbing your museum."

Clark let the words hang there for a moment to make sure they sank in. They did. The museum had never suffered a major theft as far as any of the three Gardner officials in the room knew. The only known loss had taken place more than a decade before when someone stole a miniature Rembrandt self-portrait sketch from its easel in the Dutch Room. The guard's attention had been diverted when another person smashed a bag full of lightbulbs on the marbled floors. Who stole it or why was never determined, but the etching returned just as mysteriously a few months later when a New York gallery owner was approached by a third party to buy it and saw from printing on its back that it belonged to the Gardner Museum.

The thieves FBI agent Clark was talking about had a more ambitious robbery in mind. "These are serious people, and you've got to take them seriously," he intoned ominously.

In speaking to the museum officials, he outlined several plans the FBI had vetted. The most credible, he said, involved targeting the museum during its Tuesday night concerts, held in the museum's largest single space, the Tapestry Room, which filled nearly one side of the museum's second floor.

"They're planning to set off a smoke bomb inside the Tapestry Room and, in the ensuing chaos, grab one or more of the paintings that hang on the walls of your Blue Room or Yellow Room on the first floor," Clark said.

The Yellow and Blue Room galleries were the easiest rooms to steal a painting from, since they were so close to the museum's main entrance, according to the handwritten notes of the Gardner officials during their meeting with the FBI. Raphael's *Lamentation Over the Dead Christ,* Royce's favorite painting on the desk on the second floor of the museum, was also in their sights.

"These are serious thieves," Clark told Grindle, Hadley, and Hewitt. "They have the means and know-how to carry out their plan. You've got to take appropriate measures."

"There's more," Clark said, the Gardner officials by now on the edges of their seats. "They might dress up as police officers and demand late-night entry into the museum. Or disguise themselves as women who've run into some trouble outside of the museum and ask for help and to be let in." And, perhaps most chilling of all, the pair may have a guard inside the museum who has provided them information—wittingly or unwittingly—about the security system.

"What should we be doing?" Grindle asked the agents. He had just come onto the job as the Gardner's security director and he knew, both in equipment and manpower, that the museum had a long way to go toward protecting its masterpieces.

"Well, first off, you'd better be putting more people on during those concerts," Clark snapped back. "If I know them, these guys already know the ins and outs of this place better than the mice do."

Grindle, Hadley, and Hewitt were shocked by what they'd heard. "Not sure whether it is a willing or unwitting (ac)complice," read one of their notes from the meeting. Still, they had little understanding about how aggressive Royce and his pals in the Rossetti family could be in trying to pull off this score.

Clark didn't share with the Gardner team how the FBI had learned of Royce's intention to break into the museum. But even if they'd been asked, it's unlikely that Clark would have told them anything. Even though Clark had been associating with Royce and the notorious Ralph Rossetti for months, trying to buy valuable pieces of stolen art from them as the undercover FBI agent who eventually busted them that day outside the Italian restaurant in East Boston, it was FBI protocol to provide sufficient information only for potential victims to protect themselves. So Clark wasn't authorized to share the true seriousness of the threat to the museum. Had Clark divulged what he knew, it would likely have only increased the museum's concern about Royce's ingenuity as a master thief, and his associations with the Rossettis.

Maybe it was the wrong decision. Less than ten years later, the security staff at the Isabella Stewart Gardner Museum would come to wish they'd convinced museum trustees that radical changes were needed in the security system to protect the collection. The FBI had warned them, but the museum didn't make its biggest changes until it was too late.

—————————————

FOR SEVEN YEARS after being released from the state prison in 2007, Louis Royce stayed true to his pledge to the Massachusetts parole board to stay clear of involvement in any criminal conduct or consorting with his old pals in organized crime. But in June 2014 he was sent back to prison because of a parole violation—a teenager had complained to police that Royce had made unwanted verbal advances toward him at a Quincy playground. Although Royce disputed the youth's account and was not arrested, the report was forwarded to his parole officer, who immediately ordered his return to jail pending a hearing.

Royce rejected my urging that he contest the complaint before a parole board hearing. No, he said, and waived his right for a hearing and decided to stay in prison, believing that he had built up enough "good time"—the time that gets shaved off his original sentence for abiding by the terms of his parole while he was on the street—to be released without conditions in a month or two.

"Just leave it alone," he wrote to me. "You don't know anything about prison rules." Although I was convinced he was making the wrong decision, I had gotten to know Royce well enough over the years to know when he wasn't going to budge. Royce had become more defensive in the wake of an attack he suffered about six months after he originally had been released on parole in 2007. He had been beaten up brutally inside a Quincy halfway house by another recent parolee. Typically, he first refused to press charges against his assailant or the halfway house, saying that doing so would be against his code never to snitch on another. But he relented after doctors had to perform two surgeries on his brain, and gained an $11,000 settlement from the company that owned the halfway house.

As I got to know Royce and we continued to talk about his criminal past, I became convinced that regardless of who had actually pulled off the heist and who was involved in stashing the artwork, the idea had begun with him.

By allowing me to tell his story, Royce calculates that doing so may assist in a recovery of the paintings, and if that happens he deserves a cut of whatever multimillion-dollar reward is given in exchange for their return. He still talks with friends in law enforcement, who tell him the FBI is convinced that the heist grew from his plan and was carried out by individuals within Boston's organized crime underworld. (After Royce's exploits were detailed in *Master Thieves*, federal authorities took interest in how his planning of the theft in the 1980s might have led to the 1990 heist. In September 2015 he was summoned to a federal grand jury in Boston and questioned about how he had plotted to rob the museum and with whom in the criminal world he might have shared the secrets.) Most of all, Royce is convinced that among the few people who are still alive and know anything about who pulled off the robbery is Stevie Rossetti, his old cohort whom he had told in the early 1980s of the museum's poor security.

"If it wasn't Stevie who ordered it, he passed the score on to someone who did," Royce tells me. "The only others who might have known anything are Stevie's uncle Ralph, but he died in prison in 2008, and Richie Devlin. He was killed in a gangland shooting in 1994."

Royce shrugs off the idea that the younger Rossetti, who is serving a forty-year prison sentence for participating in an armored car robbery, would give information to federal investigators to get a reduced sentence.

"Stevie's no rat," Royce almost spits at me when I ask. "He's like me. He's loyal and his word is his bond."

Still, when I press the issue, Royce writes to Stephen Rossetti asking if they can talk, but Rossetti never responds. That Rossetti wouldn't trust him upsets Royce but he receives even more disturbing news from another former member of the Rossetti gang. When Royce had been released from prison several months after the Gardner theft and returned to East Boston to try to find out who was responsible, Mark Rossetti, Stephen's cousin, alerted the FBI that Royce was asking questions about the Gardner heist.

As had happened to him when he was barely a teenager, when he learned that John Royce was not really his father, the revelation that a member of the gang to which he had shown such allegiance and loyalty had informed on him was crushing to Royce.

Royce would get a call from his parole officer, warning him that unless he wanted to be hauled back to prison on a parole violation, he needed to stay out of East Boston and away from all his past criminal contacts, including those with whom he had first discussed robbing the Gardner Museum. By 2007, what had once been a twinkle in Royce's eye had become the most notorious unsolved art theft in American history.

CHAPTER TWO

THEY KNEW EXACTLY WHAT THEY WERE DOING

IN FEBRUARY 1989, thirteen months before two men dressed as police officers drove up to the Gardner Museum, a block away a single guard was struggling to control the throng of people who were visiting a new exhibit on the second floor of Boston's Museum of Fine Arts. No one seemed to notice the two men with a baby stroller standing in front of the million-dollar Yuan vase enclosed in a glass case at the other end of the MFA gallery. And no one said anything as the men used a screwdriver to unhinge the top of the enclosure and remove the vase from its setting. Moving quickly, and without drawing attention, they then tucked the vase snugly into the stroller and walked out of the museum.

William P. McAuliffe knows firsthand the nightmare of what a security breach at a museum can bring—he owed his job as director of security at the MFA to that one in 1989.

McAuliffe took over as the MFA's security director soon after that daring heist, and right from the start he promised to get together with Lyle Grindle, the security chief of the Gardner Museum. Together they were charged with protecting some of Boston's greatest and most irreplaceable riches, and McAuliffe knew he would benefit if they compared notes. And because of the Yuan vase caper, McAuliffe knew all too well the hazards of screwing up.

He had known nothing about museum security before he applied for the job; he had spent his career in the Massachusetts state police. But he was a quick learner, having risen to second in command of the force, and quickly immersed himself in the intricacies of guarding priceless treasures. In short order he came to learn two important lessons: that a museum was most vulnerable at night, and that guards and night watchmen should always secure a supervisor's approval before making any decision.

Whether supervisor approval was required in the past is anyone's guess, but McAuliffe underscored it to the several watchmen who worked the overnight shift at the MFA.

The importance of the lesson was driven home in the pre-dawn hours of January 15, 1990. The winding streets around the Museum of Fine Arts were quiet, empty, and, with the Boston police force having just wrapped up its safety detail for the first official Martin Luther King Jr. holiday commemoration, lightly patrolled. Suddenly two men dressed in Boston police uniforms showed up at the rear entrance of the MFA and rang the buzzer.

"Boston police—open up. We're looking for someone."

A thirty-four-year-old who had been working the overnight watch shift for several years was alone manning the control room. Security at the MFA that night was heavier than usual since the museum was about to open a new exhibit of

Claude Monet's works, with dozens of his paintings on loan for the exhibit inside.

The night watchman could see clearly through the video security system that the men who had buzzed certainly looked like police officers, but he had his orders.

"I can't let anyone in," he called back on the intercom. "We've got a new procedure. No one gets in after hours without the approval of my supervisor. I've got to find him and I'll get right back to you."

"Hey, we're looking for someone," the officer said impatiently. "Let us in!"

But the night watchman had already gone off to find his supervisor, William L. Miller, who was in a faraway gallery. It took them several minutes to get back to the rear entrance of the museum, and by the time Miller arrived, the police officers had disappeared. Except for filing an "incident report" the following morning with McAuliffe, nothing more was said of the strange episode. That is, until two months later, when Boston woke up to television news bulletins that the Gardner Museum had been robbed of several major works of art, hours after the city's next holiday, St. Patrick's Day.

IN EARLY 1990, the two security directors kept their promise to each other to evaluate how secure the Gardner Museum was from theft or other catastrophes. Their tour was barely under way when, at the wooden security desk by the museum's employee entrance, McAuliffe pointed out what he saw as a major security flaw.

"Lyle, you don't have a secure control room," McAuliffe said, clearly alarmed. "Everything is right out here in the open. You need to build a control room in a place that is secret from the public, a place that isn't vulnerable to attack."

McAuliffe was right. Grindle had a suite of security controls: communication systems to connect the cadre of guards on patrol or on duty in the various galleries inside the four-story mansion; cameras watching activities at several places inside and outside the museum on a closed circuit television system, and taping those activities on a videocassette recorder; a motion detector that silently tracked the patrons as they entered and left the galleries—but they were all out in the open, and solely within reach of the lone guard who manned it. Even the main box that connected the building's fire alarm system was there.

Grindle understood perfectly well the problems McAuliffe had raised. He had been on the job at the Gardner for nearly a decade, since the early 1980s, and he was the museum's first full-time security director. In fact, security at the Gardner had been such an afterthought before he came on board that the man who held the job before him was also responsible for maintaining the grounds that surrounded the museum.

The Gardner was the first museum Grindle had worked for. A Maine native, he was a criminal justice specialist working for the consulting firm A.D. Little & Co., in Cambridge, where he'd been for more than a decade after a stint in the navy, when he heard about the opening at the museum. At the Gardner he was a no-nonsense boss and, reflecting his military training, a stickler for adhering to meeting schedules and reporting suspicious activity around the museum.

He was also known for coming down like a hammer on his team for infractions to his many rules, no matter how small. When the candy bars he'd put out for employees to buy for $1 began disappearing, he installed a hidden camera to stop the pilfering. Two security guards were caught on the video and both were suspended.

The job Grindle was hired to do, to protect the museum's priceless collection and make improvements in the museum's security system, was a nightmare assignment. The mansion that housed the museum was built at the turn of the twentieth century, and while its Venetian palazzo architecture may have been stunning to view, the building had never undergone major renovations to accommodate new electrical, plumbing, or ventilation systems. And there was the matter of Mrs. Gardner's will, which worked against such renovations, as it prohibited the museum's trustees from altering the building's galleries in any significant way. If they did, the will stipulated, the museum would become the property of Harvard University.

For several years after being hired, Grindle acclimated himself by spending his days in an office in the museum's unfinished basement. When he finally had a proper office built, it was in the "carriage house," separate from the museum's galleries, and its only security device was a telephone.

Grindle knew he had much to do to improve the museum's security. But once the FBI visited in 1981 and told him that members of one of Boston's toughest organized crime gangs were scoping out the museum for a theft, he attached a sense of urgency to his work.

"Bill, it's not like I've been sitting on my hands here," Grindle told McAuliffe the day they finally did their walkthrough of the museum. "I've made some progress, but it's not like I have all the money in the world. And I've got a board of trustees I've got to work through. Security is only one of the demands on them."

Through much of the 1980s Grindle had pleaded with the museum's board of trustees for money to improve the mansion's security systems. It wasn't that the people who ran the museum—the seven-member board of trustees (all white men) and director Roland "Bump" Hadley—were unaware that it needed major renovations. But that all took money, and there was no plan in place to raise the money, or any fervent commitment by the trustees to come up with such a plan.

In the mid-1980s, the museum was operating in the red. There simply wasn't enough money allocated to accomplish even a fraction of what Grindle knew needed to be done, never mind the additional money for other improvements, necessary as it turned out, that he hadn't even imagined. Finally, in 1986, the board voted him a million dollars for various projects. But there was just too much to do, and every job was complicated by the age of the museum building itself.

Grindle lived in fear that the museum would suffer a catastrophic loss, not from a band of thieves but from a water leak that could not be shut off because of the antiquated pipes and plumbing that ran through the building, or a fire allowed to spread because, for a few years at least, there was no central fire alarm system, only a set of battery-operated units spread throughout the museum's galleries and corridors.

Frustrated by the begging and cajoling for money to improve security, Hadley had told Grindle at one point in the mid-1980s that if he was serious, he needed to raise the funds himself. So with the assistance of an intern, Grindle wrote letters to major corporations in and around Boston seeking the funds. He raised more than $50,000, and the money was used to install a new alarm system that alerted security staff to any fires or broken windows.

At the time the museum's collection was valued in the billions of dollars. Yet, like most museums of the era, and particularly the smaller ones, the Gardner had no insurance policy in place to protect it from the loss of any of its paintings or antiques. It was considered simply too expensive to protect against such losses. During those years the museum was paying less than $25,000 a year for a range of policies, including one that protected them from liability for patrons who might slip and fall on wet surfaces.

Frustratingly, Grindle found that it was overly costly to install the wiring needed for video and electronic surveillance systems in a building constructed at the turn of the century and that was lit for the most part with gas lamps. The building even lacked central air conditioning and ventilation, which, even worse than being uncomfortable for patrons, was damaging the artwork. Many summer mornings Grindle would find some of the paintings "sweating," showing beads of condensation from the heat and humidity that had built up inside the building overnight. In some of the hotter galleries he even resorted to ordering the windows thrown open and fans brought in to cool down the rooms.

"Four hot days in a row and it gets like a pizza oven in there," Grindle told McAuliffe as they walked through the museum's venerable Blue Room. "Only our Tapestry Room, where we hold concerts, is air conditioned." The room was cooled by a twenty-ton unit that they had installed years before on the roof of the building, Grindle explained.

A museum trustee for much of the 1980s agreed that the board was slow to recognize the need to raise more money to fund renovation projects.

"We were slow, I'll admit it, to deal with things like the climate control problem, insurance, security, and the lack of space," Francis W. Hatch Jr. told me in an interview before his death in 2010. "But to us the main problem was Bump [Hadley]. He wasn't a good administrator and he didn't like anyone talking to us but him. And really, we never paid attention to him."

By the late 1980s, Grindle was back hounding the board for more money. He had commissioned a study by the well-regarded security firm Steven R. Keller & Associates. They had recommended the same thing McAuliffe had stressed: a secured control room accessible only to those with a passkey. Keller also recommended dramatic improvements to the museum's communication system, among them maintaining a sophisticated video surveillance system that kept track of not only every gallery, but also every wall in those galleries, and every corridor leading in and out of them.

But little financial help seemed to be coming. The museum was still barely scraping by on dividends and interest from Mrs. Gardner's investments to meet its $1.5 million annual budget. Certainly the money paid by patrons and visitors wasn't going to cover the bills. Having begun charging for tickets for the first time in 1977, the museum was collecting less than $400,000 a year even a decade later.

After the theft, the *Boston Globe*'s art critic wrote a searing critique of the museum's failure to raise sufficient funds during the 1980s to care for deteriorating conditions. "The truth was, though, that the museum had been in trouble long before the robbery," the article stated. "The Gardner had simply failed to keep up with standard late-20th-century museum practices. There wasn't even an adequate place for visitors to hang their coats, let alone a climate-control system to protect the museum's masterpieces from the extremes of Boston's winters and summers. The problem was a matter of money and management. The trustees, traditionally a self-perpetuating Brahmin board of seven Harvard-educated men, acted as if fund-raising were tantamount to begging. In the 1980s, when there was big money available for arts institutions, the museum didn't even apply for big grant money—at a time when the Gardner needed millions of dollars' worth of climate control and conservation."

While not disputing any statistics in the critique, Anne Hawley, then the museum's director, defended the trustees' dedication to the museum and contended the article had been motivated by the *Globe*'s anger in not getting preferential treatment in covering the theft. "First we were robbed, and then we were mugged," Hawley told the *New York Times* after the *Globe* article came out.

In 1985, after years of his badgering, Grindle and other members of the museum's senior staff finally convinced the board of the seriousness of his needs, not to mention the need to modernize the premises generally, and the museum hired a specialist in fund-raising to make recommendations. Caroline Standley, who had run a successful campaign for the Peabody Essex Museum in Salem on Massachusetts's North Shore, advised the board to reach out to well-to-do Bostonians who would certainly be willing to make annual contributions to a capital campaign for the museum.

"There are people out there who would love to support the museum and its treasures. All they need is to be asked," Standley told the board. She said she estimated that the museum would be able to raise 30–40 percent of its budget through such a campaign. But the board rejected the initiative, fearing that such members would inevitably want to have a say in the museum operations, and that might lead to a conflict with the board itself, which under Mrs. Gardner's will had to maintain sole responsibility for the museum's direction.

The Gardner's board members served unlimited terms not because of their love of art or their fund-raising prowess but because they came from the right families. They dismissed Standley's pleas out of hand.

"I do know that [the trustees] . . . pretty much wanted to stay in their own little world, which would have been fine, except the outside world was changing and the museum had these space needs that badly needed to be addressed," Standley said in an interview.

In 1987, out of frustration from trying to convince the trustees to approve a plan, Standley stepped down from her fund-raising advisory position. A year later, the museum's deputy director resigned, explaining in a letter to a board member, "I could not work effectively for the museum under the conditions of confusion, indecision, inadequate communication and a lack of defined and shared goals [among] trustees, advisory committee and staff."

The next year, in 1989, Hadley submitted his resignation, stating in a final report that he asked the board to keep confidential until 1994 that the failure to establish a fund-raising campaign had doomed him. "The campaign was ended without consulting with the staff charged with fundraising, and good faith between trustees and staff was broken. . . . Until that faith is restored the museum cannot make plans," he wrote that June. The museum was robbed less than a year later.

(Their reluctance to overspend on security did not prevent some of the trustees from trying to place blame on Grindle after the theft. At one board meeting, they pressed him on why a lock on one of the security doors the thieves had to pass through once granted access inside the museum was missing. Grindle pointed out that he had requested $500 to fix the broken lock as a prior budget request but it had never been granted.)

So in early 1990, as their tour of the Gardner building concluded, Grindle and McAuliffe shook hands and promised to keep discussing each other's security needs.

"Let's be sure to grab a drink in Chicago," Grindle said, referring to the upcoming meeting of institutional security directors in the week leading up to St. Patrick's Day weekend, 1990.

"I'VE GOT A TICKET to the Dead in Hartford tomorrow night," Rick Abath called out to his roommate as he left for work on March 17, 1990. "If I can score another ticket, I might stay for Monday's show, too."

"What about work?" Abath's roommate called back to him.

Abath went on his way, as he had done countless times in the past, checking doors and the empty galleries.

"I've already given my notice. What more can they do to me?" Abath shot back.

It was the sort of smart-ass, know-it-all response Abath was known for around the Gardner Museum, where he was a night watchman. He stood out among the staff of thirty-five security guards, most of whom were college kids or retirees on Social Security, because of his sharp tongue. Abath was also smart and known among his colleagues for persistently questioning his superiors about the museum's need to spend more money on improving security equipment and paying guards more. But after working the midnight shift for nearly a year, Abath had tired of his night watchman's job. He was tolerating it only because the job suited his casual attitude and didn't interfere too much with his real aspirations: making it in the world of rock music.

Abath's band Ukiah, a Phish knockoff, was landing a sufficient number of gigs in a few of Boston's grungier nightspots, so Abath felt sure it was only a matter of time before he could make his way as both the band's guitarist and manager, not shining flashlights into darkened corners of a small, under-appreciated Boston museum.

Grindle, the museum's security director, had hired Abath and appreciated that he had someone he could depend on to work the midnight shift. But in the months leading up to the theft, he had gotten disenchanted with the young man, who never seemed to stop complaining about the most minor of lapses and who rumor had it was showing up for work looking either stoned or tipsy. In fact, Abath had begun to slack off considerably in those final months, and admits to often being under the influence of marijuana or liquor during the nights he would rush to the museum from a Ukiah gig at a nearby club.

Grindle definitely had no idea of the little party Abath had held for a few friends at the Gardner a few months before, on New Year's Eve. Despite being strictly prohibited, Abath allowed several close friends, including two brothers who also worked at the museum, to usher in the new year with a low-key party. Abath supplied his favorite top-shelf Bombay gin.

"I figure if I have to work tonight, I'm not going to spend it without my friends," he told them as they camped out among the Gardner's masterpieces.

The incident should have cost Abath his job. But the second night watchman on duty with him that New Year's Eve liked Abath and didn't report him. In fact, that same man, Joseph M. Mulvey, Abath's regular partner and an old-timer who had been working security at the museum since the mid-1980s, was scheduled to work the overnight shift with Abath on March 18. But when Abath arrived a half hour before the shift was scheduled to start, he found that Mulvey had called in sick.

There was a scramble until Randy Hestand agreed to work the shift. Four years older than Abath, Hestand had been hired as a gallery guard at the museum the year before. That night would be the first time Hestand worked as a night watchman, but he knew the shift had long periods of down time, and he brought his trombone along with him.

"We'll alternate patrolling the galleries," Abath told Hestand, reiterating what he'd been told over the phone when he'd agreed to the shift. "It should take about an hour to complete. We document the rounds by turning our security keys in the alarm locks around the building."

While one man was doing his patrols—unarmed but carrying a flashlight and walkie-talkie—the other would sit at the security desk, where he could watch a television screen that showed the closed circuit images from four cameras around the building's perimeter. Those images were captured on a videocassette recorder located inside the small office, where the duty commander customarily sat. The only other piece of equipment, an IBM computer that registered the footsteps of anyone passing through any of the sixty motion-activated infrared sensors spread through the museum, sat close by. The security system had been installed about two years previously at a cost of about $100,000. It was turned on.

"I'll take the first patrol through the galleries," Abath told Hestand, enjoying pulling a bit of seniority on the older man. "But you see that button?" he asked, pointing to a small round button molded within arm's reach on the right side of the security desk. "That's the panic alarm. Hit that if there's any emergency, and the police will be here in minutes."

In fact, that button was the only alarm the museum had in place that could alert the outside world to a problem inside the building. While other museums had instituted a fail-safe system, which required the night watchmen to make hourly phone calls to convey that all was well, the panic button at the Gardner's front security desk was the only way to summon police to an emergency.

Abath went on his way, checking doors and the empty galleries. He was midway through his rounds when whatever hopes he had for a routine evening were shattered. Suddenly he heard the fire alarm box just a few feet away from the security desk going off loudly. While the box could pinpoint thirty places around the museum where a fire had started or a window had been broken, this time all the alarm stations throughout the building were blaring out their siren call.

"What the hell is going on down there?" Abath shouted into his two-way radio.

"You'd better get down here, Rick," Hestand said, a slight panic in his voice. "The whole box is going off."

Abath ran to the alarm box and shut it down. He reset it and then turned it on again. Once again, its bright lights lit up like a Christmas tree and the sirens wailed throughout the building.

"What the hell is wrong with it?" Hestand asked.

"I've got no idea," Abath shot back. "I've never seen anything like it."

Abath considered calling someone but decided instead to just shut down the box for the night and to make sure a repairman was summoned in the morning. Abath went back to his rounds, starting over from the beginning as his security manual required. He finally completed his tour around 1 A.M. But before he relieved Hestand at the security desk, he made a sharp detour into the anteroom between the museum itself and the outside door. The door was of heavy oak and had been the side entrance to the museum since its construction in 1903. A metal latch that was still in place had been the original mechanism for locking the door, but it now locked and unlocked electronically, with a control switch at the security desk, or manually, as Abath was about to do. Without telling Hestand what he was doing or why, Abath opened the side door and shut it again.

Outside on the street, two men in a parked car would have seen Abath open and shut the door. They'd been sitting in their dark-colored hatchback on Palace Road, about one hundred feet away from the employee entrance to the museum, for a while, and they squinted through their windows, thick with condensation from their breath that cool night. In the half hour before, the quiet on the street had been suddenly broken when a group of youthful St. Patrick's Day revelers emerged from a nearby apartment building. There were about five in all, and they were tipsy from the late-night party they'd just left. The men in the hatchback, dressed in police uniforms and wearing police caps, made no move as a couple of the kids danced around them and then climbed one another's shoulders in the middle of Palace Road.

"Cops," a girl who had climbed onto her boyfriend's shoulders for a brief wrestling match with another couple stage-whispered as she spied the two men. Through the clouded windows she saw that both men were wearing police hats and that the driver had on a coat with a police patch on its arm.

One of the revelers, Tim Conway, saw them too. He noticed their uniforms and wondered what they were doing in an unmarked car. "They've got to be doing surveillance on someone," he thought and tried to be nonchalant as he walked around to the back of the car to see if it had any medallions or a special license plate to designate it as a police vehicle. There were none.

For a second Conway considered knocking on the car's window to ask the two men what they were waiting for, but he also knew he was in no condition to be asking questions of the police. Conway had consumed much of the two six-packs of Irish beer he'd brought to the party and knew he was tipsy. To top it off he was only nineteen, well below the legal drinking age.

Conway and his friends quickly disappeared into the misty, cool night, leaving the hatchback and its two occupants alone.

A few minutes later, at 1:20 in the morning, the hatchback started up and drove slowly past the heavy oak door of the Gardner's employee entrance and parked. Inside the museum, Abath saw the car via the closed circuit television camera that hung over the door, then turned his attention elsewhere. When he looked up again, the two men, dressed in police uniforms, were at the door reaching for the buzzer.

"Police," one of the two men said, turning to look at the closed circuit television that hung over the door. "We're here about the disturbance."

Abath was unaware of any disturbance at the museum, or of any call made to 911 to report one. But he also knew that, this being St. Patrick's Day, anything might have happened on the grounds surrounding the museum and that the closed circuit televisions easily could have missed it. Perhaps someone had climbed over the iron fence and gotten into the grounds in the back of the museum, he thought. Maybe someone in the security post at Simmons College across the street had seen it and called the police.

Abath pressed the buzzer on the console at his security desk, giving the men access into the museum. As they entered the "mantrap"—the locked foyer that separated the rear door from the actual museum—he could see them clearly. One was taller than the other, and they looked to be dressed in police uniforms, right down to the union pins fastened to their shirt collars.

"Is there anyone else here with you?" the shorter of the two asked Abath.

"Just one other," Abath responded. "He's on his rounds."

"Get him down here, immediately," the short officer demanded.

Abath grabbed his walkie-talkie and called Hestand to come back to the security desk.

Just then Abath noticed that while both had mustaches, the one on the taller of the two seemed fake. In fact, it looked pasted to his face. But before he got to look more closely, the shortest of the pair leaned toward him.

"You look familiar," he said accusingly to Abath, squinting his eyes. "I think we have a warrant out for your arrest. Come out from behind the desk and show us some identification."

Abath had had no brushes with the law and knew he had no warrants, but his immediate concern was that if he didn't comply, he'd be arrested and have to spend the rest of the weekend in jail. If that happened, he knew he'd miss those Grateful Dead concerts in Hartford.

He stood up and stepped away from the security desk. It would be Abath's second grievous error in judgment. First he'd broken protocol by letting the officers into the museum. Now he was facing them, unarmed and outmanned.

In a matter of seconds the shorter man had steered Abath to a nearby wall. He forced him to spread his legs and slapped a pair of handcuffs on him.

Wait a minute, Abath thought to himself. *He didn't even frisk me.*

It was at that moment Abath knew the two men he'd let into the museum weren't police officers. They hadn't come to investigate a disturbance. They were there to rob the place, and he had allowed it to happen.

Abath had his face to the wall when Hestand walked into the room and heard him ask why he was being arrested. Out of the corner of his eye he could see that the taller of the two men had turned Hestand around and was putting handcuffs on him.

"This is a robbery, gentlemen," one of the men said almost matter-of-factly. "Don't give us any problems, and you won't get hurt."

"Don't worry," Abath responded sharply. "They don't pay me enough to get hurt."

The thieves quickly wrapped both men in large strips of the duct tape they'd brought in with them, covering even the watchmen's heads and eyes. Then, without asking how to get there, the two men led the hapless guards to the basement. They seated Hestand beside an unused sink, which he was then handcuffed to. Abath was led down a long, narrow corridor to a workbench, where the intruders seated and handcuffed him as well.

After relieving them of their wallets, the thieves told each man, "We know where you live now. Do as we tell you and no harm will come to you. If you don't tell them anything, you'll get a reward from us in about a year."

You people have no interest in doing anything for me now or a year from now, Abath thought to himself, as he tried to relax as best he could, getting accustomed to being handcuffed to the sink with the duct tape still covering his eyes and face.

While the thieves went about wreaking havoc inside the museum, Abath's mental state went from boredom to terror. He knew these guys were serious and that they certainly didn't intend to get caught. With that in mind, Abath figured they'd likely set fire to the place before they left, and he began to panic. He began to sing, almost chant, Bob Dylan's "I Shall Be Released" over and over again: "So I remember every face, of every man who put me here."

Even so, when Boston police later asked him what the men looked like, Abath could provide only the sketchiest of details. One of the thieves appeared to be in his late thirties. About five feet, nine inches, slim with gold wire glasses and a mustache, though that was probably fake. The other looked to be in his early thirties, six feet tall and heavier, with chubby cheeks. He also sported a mustache.

"That's awful!" Abath blurted out when the police showed him the artist's composite drawing based on the description he'd provided. In the ensuing years all he could remember was that one of the men looked like Colonel Klink from the popular late '60s television show *Hogan's Heroes.*

But sitting there handcuffed, helpless while the intruders were doing God knows what, all Abath could do was cycle through his mind, wondering if he had ever seen either of the pair before. Maybe he'd spoken to them in a bar or some other chance encounter and told the thieves about the museum's miserable security system. Or maybe it was because so many people had worked the night shift over the years and knew the terrible secret that there was only one alarm to alert the outside world of a problem inside the museum and that the next shift didn't start until 6:30 the next morning, so there was no one to check on things once Abath and Hestand had been subdued.

The FBI and Boston police artist drew sketches of the two robbers following the heist using recollections of the two night watchmen who were on duty. However, more recently the security officer who spent the most time with the thieves dismissed the accuracy of the images.

It could have been anybody, Abath thought. How many times had he and his roommates—several of whom also worked security at the Gardner—complained to each other about the lousy security the museum had in place?

Abath had probably made such claims in his own house, which was less than two blocks away from an antiques store run by a suspicious character with mob ties. William Youngworth, the store owner, was a friend of several members of the Rossetti gang, and would draw much attention to himself in 1997 by claiming he could facilitate the return of the stolen artwork. Had Abath's complaints—which suddenly seemed to him to be very conspicuous, and perhaps even a threat to his life—somehow been overheard by Youngworth? Or perhaps Abath shot off his mouth about the museum's security lapses at the Channel, a rock club Abath remembers visiting, or one of the seedier ones where Ukiah played in Brighton or other Boston neighborhoods, some of which had mob connections of varying degrees.

All these thoughts tumbled through Abath's mind as he lay handcuffed and covered in duct tape in the museum basement.

It had taken the thieves about fifteen minutes to subdue Abath and Hestand. It was 1:35 A.M. While Abath sat imagining these conspiracies, the thieves were on their way, moving among the Gardner's hallowed galleries.

Strangely, their first footsteps weren't picked up on the museum's motion detector until they made their way to the Dutch Room on the second floor at 1:48. The pair may have waited to make sure their presence inside the museum hadn't been detected and that no emergency calls had been made to the Boston PD. Most important, they made sure no cruisers had been sent to investigate.

Surely they also had knowledge about the museum's security system and layout. They knew they had to get Abath away from the panic button located within his reach at the security desk. They knew how to get to the museum's basement and where to hold Abath and Hestand. Now they knew police had no way of knowing that the heist was under way.

The Gardner was theirs. They could have spent the entire night inside.

"Someone is in the Dutch Room. Investigate immediately." At 1:51 A.M. the motion detector on the first floor typed out that message, but of course no one was there to see it. The two intruders had made their way up the Gardner's marble steps to the second floor and had entered the gallery where some of Mrs. Gardner's richest treasures were kept: three large Rembrandts and Vermeer's *The Concert*.

The Storm on the Sea of Galilee was the most valuable of the Rembrandts that Mrs. Gardner had purchased for her museum. The only seascape the master is known to have done, the painting is a dramatic representation of the story told in Luke's chapter in the New Testament of the Bible of Christ calming a violent storm that has so frightened his disciples they awoke him. Regarded as an important work from his early period, Rembrandt was seemingly so impressed with the painting that he included an image of himself, leaning over the side of the boat with a harrowed look on his face, in the work. Mrs. Gardner purchased the painting from a London gallery in 1898 for $125,000 after learning of its availability from Bernard Berenson, the young Harvard-educated art specialist she'd hired to locate masterpieces to fill the galleries she envisioned sharing with the world. Estimates have placed its value at over $100 million since its theft.

The painting itself was large, at more than five feet in length and four feet in width, and even bigger encased in a golden frame. Hardly master thieves, the intruders pulled the majestic Rembrandt from where it hung on the far wall of the gallery and threw it to the marbled floor, shattering the glass in the huge frame. With its canvas exposed, they cut the painting, which had been completed in 1633, sharply from its wooden backing.

As they did, a small device suddenly began to screech from a socket on a nearby wall. The size of a night light, the device had been installed to warn the Dutch Room gallery guard that a patron had gotten too close to the canvas, most often to point out that Rembrandt had etched an image of himself among the disciples on the boat. The sound likely shocked the pair, and one of them hunted it down and smashed it to pieces.

Again there was silence.

They were just as brutal with the second Rembrandt, *A Lady and Gentleman in Black*. The two broke its enormous glass frame, cutting it from its wooden backing, too. Although not as dramatic a sight as *The Storm on the Sea of Galilee*, the painting originally included a young boy waving a wand or stick to the lady's right. But the figure was removed when the work was completed in 1633.

The thieves then moved on to a third large Rembrandt, a self-portrait of the Dutch master. Deciding it was too large to transport, the pair left it leaning against a cabinet rather than making off with it. While that self-portrait may have been too large to transport, the thieves did grab a postage stamp–size portrait Rembrandt had etched of himself from the table beneath it. Remarkably, it was the second time the work had been snatched.

In the only other theft known to have taken place at the museum, the self-portrait had been stolen in a daytime heist in 1970 when a patron diverted a guard's attention by throwing a bag filled with lightbulbs onto the floor, making a loud crash, and an accomplice snatched the self-portrait from its stand. Although no one was ever arrested in the theft, the drawing was returned to the museum several months later by an art dealer who told authorities that an unknown person had come in to sell it to him, but when the gallery noticed on its back a stamp that showed it belonged to the Gardner, he called the museum immediately to report its whereabouts.

Now, two decades later, a far bigger robbery was taking place. The thieves then moved to a small table on the right side of the gallery and concentrated on the two paintings atop it: Vermeer's *The Concert* and a painting that had long been regarded as being by Rembrandt, the pastoral scene *Landscape with an Obelisk*. *The Concert* was by far the most valuable of the thirteen pieces ultimately taken that night. Only 28½ by 25½ inches, the painting is said to have been Mrs. Gardner's first acquisition of a major artwork, purchased at a Paris auction for $5,000 in 1892. Its value is now estimated at $250 million, more than $100 million higher than the 2013 sale of Francis Bacon's triptych, *Three Studies of Lucian Freud,* by Christie's New York. Vermeer's masterwork fully displays his uncanny ability to capture light and dark in great detail. *The Concert* shows a man and two women playing music, with the late-day light softly entering the room through a window on the left, and casting a different glow to every inch of the oriental rug lying atop a table and every fold of the women's dresses. Its brilliant whites capture the small strands of pearls each woman wears.

Without regard for any of this, the thieves removed the great work from its golden frame. Then they did the same to *Landscape with an Obelisk*, which rested at the other end of the table in the Gardner's Dutch Room. It has long mystified many as to why this work was among the pieces the thieves took, as it had long before been dismissed as a painting by Rembrandt.

It's also a mystery as to why the thieves decided to take the final piece they did from the Dutch Room: a Chinese beaker from the Shang era. Called a *ku*, the foot-tall vase was one of the oldest artifacts in the museum, dating back to 1200 BC, with its worth estimated at several thousand dollars.

The thieves spent sixteen minutes inside the Dutch Room, mostly dashing back and forth from it to the Short Gallery on the other end of the second floor. There, although a priceless Michelangelo drawing was nearby, the thieves concentrated their attention on a Napoleonic banner. They labored to get the banner out of the glass-and-wood frame that encased it on a four-foot flagpole at the far end of the gallery. The frame was fastened together by six tiny screws, and the thieves removed them, dropping each to the floor below. The task proved too laborious, however, and the pair finally abandoned the job. But before they jumped down from their perch, they snatched the gold-plated eagle—called a finial—that rested atop the flagpole.

Upon climbing down, frustrated by their failure, they turned their ire to two frames in a nearby case that contained five sketches by Edgar Degas. Smashing both frames, they tore the sketches from them. Whether the thieves were interested in the horseracing motif of the sketches or angry at their inability to free the Napoleonic banner, the combined value of the Degas sketches was less than $100,000.

"To me it's the biggest mystery in the entire case," says Anthony Amore, the security director of the museum, who has

Crime scene photos taken after the theft. (1) The havoc of the theft is shown in the second-floor Dutch Room, where the greatest masterpieces were taken, leaving behind broken frames and shattered glass. (2) Richard Abath, who made the grievous error of allowing the thieves into the museum. (3) The frame of Eduard Manet's *Chez Tortoni,* taken from the first floor Blue Room, was left on the chair of the museum's security chief. (4) Five prints by Edgar Degas were broken from frames that hung in the Short Gallery.

long analyzed every move the thieves made, baffled by how they decided what to take. "Why did they take what they did, and leave what they did? It just makes no sense to me."

The Gardner Museum contained extraordinary master-works like Titian's *Rape of Europa,* said to be the single most valuable painting in all of Boston, but the thieves never went near it, or anything else on the third floor of the museum, for that matter.

Most baffling was the final painting stolen: Edouard Manet's *Chez Tortoni.* It lay on a table in the Blue Room, on the first floor of the museum, beneath a better-known Manet portrait: one of the painter's mother. Even more mystifying than the thieves' choice of that painting was that the Gard-ner's motion detectors—which had picked up every step the thieves made that night—didn't show any footsteps leading into, out of, or even inside the Blue Room. With an infrared sensor covering the expanse of the smaller Blue Room, no sign that the thieves set foot in the gallery has ever emerged. In fact, the only footsteps the equipment picked up going through the Blue Room that night were Abath's, during the two times he passed through the gallery on his patrol earlier in the evening.

Several weeks after the theft, museum security consultant Steven Keller was called in to review the aftermath and con-cluded that the Aerotech motion detector equipment the mu-seum used had worked fine the night of the heist. Keller said he tested the equipment himself, trying to avert detection by tiptoeing around the presumed placement of the sensors and crawling on the floor. He failed with every attempt, leaving him with only one explanation: that the Manet had been taken by someone other than the thieves.

Because of Abath's conduct and the spate of curious ac-tions that night, investigators have remained suspicious of him and kept open the possibility that he was somehow involved in the scheme. They point out that in 80 percent of major art heists, the thieves have had the assistance of an insider at the museum. It made sense given his friction with Grindle; Abath might have had something to do with the heist. Even the thieves' final act before leaving the museum, dropping the gold frame in which the Manet had been set on the chair Grindle used in the makeshift office behind the security desk, had the feel of a final insult toward Grindle.

In 2010 Abath was called before a grand jury, where he admitted to investigators that he prided himself on being able to avoid having his footsteps picked up on the motion detector equipment by "duck walking" through a gallery, like rocker Chuck Berry. But he insisted he had had nothing to do with the thieves or the theft itself, and reminded the grand jurors that he had remained duct-taped and handcuffed in the basement the entire night.

The thieves didn't need any help from him, Abath later told me: "They knew exactly what they were doing."

But nearly twenty years after the theft, two FBI agents suddenly appeared in the Vermont town where Abath lives with his wife and two sons from a previous marriage.

"You know we've never lost sight of you, never been able to eliminate you as a suspect," the agents told him. "We've kept an eye on your bank account even."

"I passed your stupid lie detector tests," Abath reminded them, referring to the two tests he'd passed soon after the robbery in which he was pressed about any involvement in the heist or associations he may have had with the thieves. While not entirely true—Abath had said he failed a question on the first exam, when he answered "no" to whether he had taken any drugs within forty-eight hours of taking the test— during the second examination, after the FBI's polygraph specialist had advised him to skip the question about drugs, Abath said he did pass with flying colors. (An investigator familiar with Abath's tests would not comment for this book, but shook his head no when asked whether Abath was describing the results of his polygraph correctly.)

Besides, Abath has lived a threadbare lifestyle, in Portland, Oregon, where he moved a year or so after the theft, and later in Vermont, where he and his wife have lived for more than a decade. More than anything else, his modest existence is the most convincing proof that Abath's culpability stems from negligence rather than any role as an accomplice.

Yet the man who trained Abath for the night watchman's position says his story doesn't add up. JonPaul Kroger insists that Abath had been told specifically to be skeptical of anyone who sought entry into the museum after hours, even if they identified themselves as police officers. In fact, in such events, the night watchmen were trained to take down the names and badge numbers and phone Boston police headquarters to confirm that the officers had actually been dispatched to the museum.

"It was something I was taught when I did that shift," Kroger says. "And it was something that I stressed when I taught Abath and others like him."

Also, Kroger insists that everyone who manned the security desk knew that the only way to summon the outside world to an emergency inside the museum was through the alarm buzzer behind the desk.

"To have walked away from that buzzer is beyond negligent," Kroger says ruefully. "Really it was foolhardy, but then that was Rick."

Furthermore, Abath was unreliable. Kroger says Abath was often late or called in sick, saying he was ill or too inebriated to work.

Most disturbingly, Kroger casts doubt on Abath's explanation for why he opened the museum's outside door before taking over the security desk to begin his night's work, as the computer printout showed he did a few minutes before the thieves showed up. Abath, for his part, contends that he did it routinely to make sure the outside door was locked, and contrary to some speculation, it certainly was not meant as a sign to the robbers that they could begin their theft.

Kroger insists that the computer printout was checked every day by security supervisors and that if Abath had been opening the side door on a routine basis, the supervisors would have quickly detected it as a security breach and stopped it. Kroger is adamant that all night watchmen were trained never to open the museum door except in case of an extreme emergency, such as a fire.

As for the FBI, it took possession of all the museum's security equipment and surveillance reports soon after the robbery and has declined to answer questions about Abath's actions that night or on prior shifts. But in August 2015, the FBI and US attorney's office in Boston released a videotape that raised doubts about Abath's claimed vigilance to his job's duties and his lack of familiarity with the thieves.

Taken by the museum's in-house video surveillance system the night before the theft, the six-minute tape drew front-page attention in newspapers in Boston and across the country. It showed Abath buzzing a stranger, who had driven up in a car that appeared to look like a hatchback, into the museum and chatting with him amiably at the security desk. Who was the stranger, and was his stay inside the museum, which lasted about three minutes, a "run-through" for the next night's events?

In releasing the tape, US attorney Carmen Ortiz asked for the public's help to answer those questions but, more than a month later, Gardner's current security director Amore, who has worked closely with investigators, said the FBI had still not been able to identify the stranger.

But a key question—why it took twenty-five years to release the contents of the videotape—drew no definitive answers. Vincent Lisi, the outgoing head of the FBI's Boston office, contended in an interview with *Globe* columnist Kevin Cullen that his agents had long known they had possession of the tape but he didn't say they had actually watched it and pursued what it showed. Former museum security officials said the first they heard of what was on the tape came in spring

2015, when they were called in by the federal prosecutor who had taken over the investigation and questioned its contents. The delay in pursuing the tape's contents has had one definite consequence—it's made reasonable the explanation Abath has given to investigators who grilled him about why he violated Gardner's security protocol the night before the theft by allowing a stranger into the museum. Abath told the investigators he had no memory of the incident and did not recognize the stranger, according to a *Globe* report on his interrogation.

The FBI was said to have been furious with the decision by Ortiz's office to release the tape, knowing it raised the real implication that its investigators had been negligent in not pursuing its contents far earlier. Whether the agents diligently tracked leads that came in as a result of the release is uncertain. A former Massachusetts prosecutor said agents never contacted him after he told the press that he had relayed to investigators that a former client of his could identify the visitor.

Also, a former museum guard told me she had never heard back from the FBI's Boston office after she called in a tip saying she recognized the "stranger"—it was the Gardner's deputy security chief, Larry O'Brien, who had returned to the museum after midnight, she thought, to retrieve his wallet that he had left there the day before. The FBI dismissed her contention, but three former security guards who worked at the museum at the time of the theft agreed with her wholeheartedly—the "stranger" looked exactly like O'Brien. And a check of state motor vehicles record showed that at the time he owned the same make and model of car—1982 Ford Escort hatchback—that the FBI believed was seen driving up to the museum's side entrance in the tape. O'Brien died in 2014 and neither his brother nor Grindle, the museum's then-security director, could confirm the tip about the stranger's identity. But both Grindle and O'Brien's brother also said they had never been contacted by the FBI following the guard's tip, which, if true, would remove the suspicion that Abath had violated museum protocol exactly twenty-four hours before the theft by allowing an "unauthorized visitor" into the museum.

Abath says that while it was preposterous to think so, he always had in the back of his mind that perhaps the thieves would return someday and provide him a reward as they had promised, to show their appreciation for being so compliant during the robbery. And when he found a package of marijuana in an alley near his Brighton home several months later, he took it as a possible gesture from the thieves and he stopped his daydreaming. No one was ever coming back to thank him and he was lucky to be alive.

Although he acknowledges that he made errors in judgment that allowed the theft to take place, Abath does not blame himself. Instead, he said he should have been better trained by his superiors.

Before the thieves left the building, one of them made his way back down the cellar stairs to check on Abath and Hestand. Abath says he could hear the thief breathing steadily, standing there just watching him. Then the thieves left.

With their small hatchback waiting outside the museum, the thieves didn't bother to take everything they had stolen in one haul. At 2:40 A.M., both sets of doors were opened, and then closed again just a minute later. Five minutes later, at 2:45 A.M., both sets of doors opened and shut again. The men must have left separately five minutes apart, each carrying a portion of the stolen artwork. Were they able to get all thirteen pieces into the confines of the small hatchback they had been seen sitting in minutes before the robbery? Or had a second vehicle met them outside of the Palace Road entrance to help them? Like so much else they did that night, the question remains unanswered. Just as mysteriously as they'd arrived, the men disappeared into Boston's still misty night.

FOUR HOURS LATER, the two security guards who were to take over for Abath and Hestand arrived at the Palace Road entrance to the Gardner Museum and rang the bell. There was no response, and the pair didn't have a key. One of the reliefs ran to a nearby pay phone and she called Larry O'Brien, the museum's deputy director of security, at his home in nearby Somerville.

O'Brien was there in ten minutes. As soon as he entered the museum through a rear door, he noticed a first sign that something was terribly wrong: A clothes hanger, unwound to its full length, was lying at the foot of the candy machine near the rear entrance. Director Anne Hawley was a stickler for keeping the museum clean and debris-free, and O'Brien knew she would have suspended anyone who left a hanger lying there like that, let alone if they'd left it after using it to steal from the candy machine. Had the thieves gotten hungry while pulling off the greatest art heist in American history? O'Brien would later wonder if the famous score had included not only the Rembrandts and the Vermeer but a few candy bars as well.

Finally, making his way to the security desk, O'Brien realized something much more serious had taken place. His two night watchmen were missing and not responding to his calls on the museum's two-way radio system, and there, on the chair behind the desk in the makeshift supervisor's office behind the security desk, lay the empty frame that had once showcased *Chez Tortoni*, one of Manet's finest works.

O'Brien immediately found a phone. He dialed Lyle Grindle at his home.

"Lyle, you'd better get in here immediately," he shouted. "I can't find our security men and there's sure sign there's been a break-in." What he didn't tell Grindle was that he feared the thieves were still inside the museum and that the night watchmen were dead.

"Call the police right now, and don't touch anything," Grindle said, clearly shocked. "I'll be right in."

BOSTON POLICE SERGEANT ROBIN DEMARCO and Lieutenant Trent Holland were in the midst of picking up their breakfast of egg sandwiches and coffee when they received the emergency call. With sirens blazing, they drove quickly to the Gardner, where two rookie police officers and Lieutenant Patrick Cullity, the patrol supervisor for the district, joined them.

All these years on the force, and I never knew this was a museum, Cullity thought to himself as he arrived at the scene of the burglary. *I always thought it was a big house.*

Inside, the officers were met by O'Brien. He told them immediately that he feared the thieves might still be inside the museum and that the overnight guards were missing.

"I think they might be dead," he told Cullity.

As lead supervisor, Cullity took control of the scene and ordered the two rookie officers—Dan Rice, a former standout college football player, and Kenny Hearns—to begin searching in the basement while he and DeMarco went looking through the upper floors, making their way through the darkened galleries with their flashlights.

"Jesus, look at this," Cullity said to DeMarco when they reached the Dutch Room on the second floor. The beam of his flashlight caught the shards of broken glass and broken frames that had been left on the floor. "What did these people do here?"

"Lieutenant, I think we've found something down here in the cellar," Rice radioed. "Can you get down here right away?"

There, seated on a perch, still handcuffed, with his shoulder-length curly hair nearly completely wrapped in duct tape, sat Rick Abath. Hestand, too, was nearby.

"We're Boston police," Cullity told them. "Just sit there a couple of seconds longer; our police photographer is on his way and we don't want to touch or change anything until he gets his pictures."

Abath was dumbfounded by the request, but happy to have been found and alive. He sat by quietly but began to fume when one of the officers told him they would have to cut some of his hair to get the duct tape off.

Upstairs, Gardner director Anne Hawley had arrived and was trying to understand the full extent of what had happened. That would not happen until midday, after her conservator had been allowed under police guard to tour the galleries to assess what had been stolen. But standing there on the first floor, having just arrived after Grindle's near-frantic call, she shook her head in sadness as the police told of the lost Rembrandts and Vermeer.

"If I had only followed my instincts, I would have been able to stop this from ever happening," she told Grindle. "I left my party last night early enough and I wanted to come over here to get some work done. I'm thinking now I would have walked in on them as they were doing this. I don't care what would have happened to me if I could have prevented this."

By mid-afternoon, having been questioned for several hours, first by Boston police detectives and then by a swarm of agents from the FBI's Boston office who had already taken over the investigation, Rick Abath was told he could go home. When he got to the head of the three floors of stairs that wound up the inside of the house he shared, he shouted out to his roommate and fellow night watchman, John Murray.

"John, it happened. Everything we warned them about. It happened. Good luck working tonight!"

Then, as he had been planning for weeks, he got in a borrowed van and drove to Hartford to see the Grateful Dead.

Abath did not understand the size of the robbery or what had been stolen until he read the headlines the next morning coming out of his hotel in Hartford. Realizing immediately that he had to be considered an accomplice, and that his leaving the city would raise deeper questions, Abath abandoned any plan he had to stay to see the band's second performance that night and drove quickly back to Boston.

PART II
THE SEARCH

CHAPTER THREE

WE'VE SEEN IT

THERE IS LITTLE DOUBT that William P. Youngworth was an unreliable source. A petty criminal and a drug abuser, he was known to exaggerate if not outright lie in almost every dealing he had, whether it was with fellow criminals, the police, or reporters. There was perhaps no one he might have misled as prominently as Tom Mashberg, an experienced journalist with a top-notch reputation during his stints at the *New York Times*, the *Boston Globe*, and the *Boston Herald*. By the time Youngworth and Mashberg came in contact, the Gardner's works had been missing for over seven years. Youngworth could have been the key to cracking the Gardner case, providing him with the story of a lifetime in the process.

Stories abound about how Mashberg was blindfolded by strangers—he had not been—and driven to a secluded warehouse 45 minutes outside of Boston in fear for his life to see the stolen Gardner paintings. Elements of this story are true—but one critical detail, that the proximity of the warehouse was close to Boston, is simply wrong.

Mashberg began dealing with Youngworth in July 1997, after local police and FBI agents raided Youngworth's house in the suburb of Randolph, Massachusetts. Mashberg got hold of the FBI report authorizing the raid on the house, which doubled as an antique furniture outlet, and in it Boston FBI agent Neil P. Cronin wrote that he believed Youngworth "could assist with the recovery" of the Gardner paintings. Youngworth had been under FBI surveillance for several months before the raid.

That was an intriguing possibility for Mashberg, as Youngworth was close to longtime New England art thief Myles J. Connor Jr., who had stolen a Rembrandt from the Museum of Fine Arts in 1973. In the mid-1970s, Connor had also stolen from the Massachusetts State House a document of great historical value known as the Massachusetts Bay Colony Charter.

The charter was recovered in a raid on one of Connor's stash houses several months after it was stolen—but the charter was missing the 370-year-old royal wax seal that King Charles I had affixed to the document. That seal was recovered in the raid on Youngworth's house more than twenty years later, in 1997, which focused Mashberg's attention on Connor and Youngworth. Connor was behind bars serving a ten-year prison sentence for cocaine trafficking. Mashberg said he soon learned that Youngworth had secretly stored virtually all of Connor's possessions, including items Connor had stolen from museums through the years, inside Youngworth's rambling house in Randolph.

"I was exploring the idea that Youngworth had found some of the Gardner loot among Myles's possessions."

Mashberg met Youngworth while Youngworth was out on bail awaiting charges related to illegal firearms police had found during the raid on his house. The firearms were in fact three antique pistols with no firing mechanisms, and it seemed clear to Mashberg that law enforcement officials wanted to squeeze Youngworth for information on the Gardner paintings. He wrote several articles in July and early August about

Youngworth, Connor, and the new Gardner lead the FBI was pursuing.

In mid-August 1997, Mashberg received a call at his desk at the *Herald*. It was Youngworth. Mashberg was startled when Youngworth came right out and said what he'd been hinting at for some time: that he had proof that, if certain conditions were met, he could facilitate the return of the Gardner paintings to the museum.

"What are you doing tonight?" Youngworth asked him.

"Putting out the paper. They called me in on my day off because the other guy is on vacation," Mashberg responded, reminding Youngworth that as Sunday editor he was usually off Sundays and Mondays.

"Forget that," Youngworth scoffed. "I'll be there at midnight. Let's take a ride."

That night, Youngworth pulled up in front of the *Herald* driving a late-model Ford Crown Victoria. They began driving south. Mashberg had met with Youngworth a few times that month already and knew that the crook liked calling the shots, and would stonewall if Mashberg tried to cajole him into giving up information he didn't want to make known—or at least wasn't ready to just yet.

Like many ne'er-do-wells, Youngworth had unpredictable moods. That night he was alternately sullen and violently angry, spewing venom about gun possession charges that had been filed against him earlier in the month. To Mashberg, he also seemed to be strung out on drugs, in bad need of a fix.

Youngworth ranted that he wasn't going to play into the FBI's hands and give up the Gardner paintings without getting something in return. He wanted concessions, including immunity from prosecution for any crimes related to the Gardner heist, before he would agree to turn anything over. There was also the matter of a stolen van that had been found in the driveway of Youngworth's home in Randolph. Inside it authorities had found the remnants of a joint. If the gun charges fizzled, the authorities could always use the stolen vehicle charge to pressure Youngworth into cooperating.

"They know I had nothing to do with that van, or the roach," Youngworth shouted. "They've just figured out that I'm telling the truth about the paintings and they're trying to squeeze me."

It took Youngworth a while to get around to telling Mashberg where they were headed, and as the turnpike signs flashed past, the journalist got more and more anxious. Finally Youngworth told him: They were bound for Brooklyn.

"What's in Brooklyn?" Mashberg asked.

"You'll see for yourself," Youngworth shot back. "You want something to prove I'm for real? Well, I'm going to show you I'm for real."

Mashberg had noticed they were being tailed by another car and he also, finally, got Youngworth to acknowledge that the second car was being driven by his wife, Judy.

Mashberg knew Youngworth couldn't go much longer without a heroin fix and, regardless of what else they were going to do in Brooklyn, he also knew that Youngworth would stop somewhere to buy drugs.

What have I gotten myself into? he wondered to himself. *How do I explain this if the police pull us over, and he's high on drugs or has something stashed away in here?*

It was still dark when Youngworth pulled the Crown Victoria into the Red Hook neighborhood of Brooklyn and parked outside a housing project. Mashberg sat and waited for what seemed like an eternity, but after about half an hour Youngworth emerged, seeming calmer and even refreshed.

He's gotten himself a fix, Mashberg thought.

Within minutes, they'd pulled into the nearby parking lot of a giant warehouse on Clinton Street, directly behind the Red Hook Post Office. It was dark, and with a flashlight guiding their way they climbed the three flights of stairs to a storage unit midway down one of the corridors. Youngworth opened

A storage unit in Brooklyn's Red Hook neighborhood was the site in August 1997 where antiques dealer William Youngworth showed *Boston Herald* reporter Tom Mashberg a painting purported to be the stolen Rembrandt seascape. Authorities later claimed it was a fake.

the door with a second key and directed Mashberg to stand by the doorway.

Inside, in the dim light, Mashberg could make out a large bin about ten feet away containing several big cylinder tubes. Youngworth walked over and pulled one out, took off its large plastic top, and removed a large painting from inside it. He unfurled it, rolling it out so it hit the floor. Then he held it up higher so Mashberg could see the whole thing.

"Let me show you something," Youngworth said, breaking the eerie silence. From five feet away, with Youngworth directing his flashlight over the enormous canvas, Mashberg saw the instantly recognizable features: the sail, the waves, the figures. He couldn't make out brushstrokes, but there was cracking along the canvas throughout. The edges weren't frayed but cleanly cut.

Among the few disclosures the museum made following the theft was that the two large Rembrandts had been cut cleanly from their stretchers and frames, with only a few frayed edges.

"See the signature," Youngworth said, pointing the flashlight.

Amazed by what he was seeing, and believing it was Rembrandt's masterpiece, the seascape that had been missing for more than seven years, Mashberg edged forward to where Youngworth was standing, holding the painting above his shoulders.

"Don't get any closer," Youngworth warned him, and with that he shut off the flashlight and rolled the painting up and back into its tube.

In all, Mashberg saw the painting for about two minutes. Nine days later he broke his story on the front page of the *Boston Herald*: "WE'VE SEEN IT: Informant Shows Reporter Apparent Stolen Masterpiece."

It read, in part: "The vivid oil-on-canvas masterwork—Rembrandt's only seascape—was rolled up carefully and stored in an oversized heavy-duty poster tube with two airtight end caps at a hiding place in a barren and forsaken Northeast warehouse district.

"Under the soft glow of a flashlight, the painting was delicately pulled out and unfurled by the informant and shown to a reporter during the predawn hours of Aug. 18.

"The furtive viewing was offered to the *Herald* as proof that the paintings, stolen on March 18, 1990, from the Gardner Museum in Boston, are here in the United States—ransomable for reward money and immunity from prosecution.

"This reporter was unable to verify that the painting was the original. But the work, which was flaking slightly and somewhat frayed at the edges where it would have been cut from its frame during the Gardner heist, bore the Dutch master's signature on the ship's rudder."

Quoting his "informant" (presumably Youngworth), Mashberg's *Herald* article stated that the robbery had been pulled off by five men, only two of whom were identified: Robert A. (Bobby) Donati, who was one of the two robbers who entered the museum, and David A. Houghton, who was responsible for moving the stolen art to a safe house. Both Donati and Houghton were dead when the article was published, and none of the other three men were identified.

A few days later, Mashberg was summoned to meet with museum director Anne Hawley and other museum officials.

"What do you feel the likelihood is that you saw the real thing, the stolen Rembrandt?" Hawley asked point-blank. Mashberg didn't hesitate.

"On a scale of one to ten, I'd say close to a ten," Mashberg responded. Later that day, the museum put out a statement saying that what Mashberg saw could be "either the original or a close replica."

In the near quarter-century since the theft, Mashberg's viewing, which he walked me through in a three-hour, on-the-record interview, remains the most authoritative statement by a credible source that any of the thirteen stolen paintings had been seen. Yet the account has been subsequently tarnished: Federal authorities tested paint chips Youngworth supplied to Mashberg to verify his story, and found them to be clearly dated from Rembrandt's era (seventeenth century) but not a match to *The Storm on the Sea of Galilee*. The museum's security director argued that the heavily varnished Rembrandt painting could not have been unfurled in the way Mashberg described. Even Mashberg now doubts that what he saw was in fact *The Storm on the Sea of Galilee*. Perhaps it was just a very good replica.

"My doubt comes from [the fact that] nothing ever came of it," Mashberg said in a recent interview. "Here was the painting literally seeming like it was inches away from being recovered, then, poof, it's gone and the whole potential scenario is wiped out, and everybody off on other trails. I know what I saw but if I am getting dubious responses, then I have to own to the possibility that I was wrong."

Mashberg's bombshell article, which strongly implied that Youngworth had arranged the viewing, touched off a mad scramble by FBI agents and federal prosecutors. They tried to convince Youngworth to explain to them how he had arranged the viewing, how he might have gotten his hands on the painting, and if nothing else, where the viewing had taken place. But Youngworth held firm: He would cooperate only if all of his demands for immunity—dropping of the charges against him and releasing his friend, the master art thief Myles Connor, who was serving time in federal prison on drug-related charges—were granted.

But while numerous other lowlifes like Youngworth had sought money from the museum on the pledge that they could produce the missing paintings, this junkie-criminal now had something none of them did: credibility.

Youngworth met with Hawley, museum trustee Arnold Hiatt, and several other museum officials, and traded on that credibility. He asked for $10,000 so he could continue his pursuit of the artwork. Hiatt gave him the money as a loan. It was never repaid, and for his generosity Hiatt was subpoenaed to testify along with Hawley before a federal grand jury on whether Youngworth had coerced the money out of him.

Meanwhile, Youngworth refused to give investigators, museum officials, or Mashberg any details about how he got his hands on the stolen Rembrandt. He cryptically suggested to Mashberg in a note that his connections inside Boston's underworld, specifically his ties to the Rossetti gang in East Boston, had played a role, not to mention that Youngworth's sister had dated a member of the gang.

The note was confusingly worded and has long been scrutinized for information. It stated in part: "You have to remember the Salemme's visitation power had to be endorsed by NY. Had it not been, NY would have taken the whole as they are now going to and so I don't know power. . . . But Bobby D. was about a centimeter away from being made. And they clipped him. They were all rough. Not one of them were made. Richie D. recruited that crew in Walpole, with exception of Ritchie Gillis and he is first cousin to the Rossettis. And that's how he got in."

Here's one way of interpreting what the note said: The New York underworld had given Frank Salemme, whom the Rossetti gang reported to, approval for Youngworth to be allowed to take Mashberg to see the painting. Those New York mobsters were now going to take possession of the paintings. Donati had been killed just before he was to be inducted as a made member of the mafia. The crew, presumably who pulled off the Gardner heist, had been put together by Richard Devlin, another member of the Rossetti crew, while serving time in Walpole prison. Richard Gillis, a cousin to the Rossettis, had been an original member of either the Rossetti gang or those who had pulled off the robbery.

But Youngworth went on in the note to stress that Mashberg needed to be extra careful in dealing with anyone in the Rossetti gang. He told of his involvement with the heist of a truckload of oriental rugs in Manchester, New Hampshire, in 1981, which had ended with Rossetti gang members shooting two of the truck drivers. Youngworth told Massachusetts state police that hours after that shooting he and his best friend had been summoned to meet with several involved in the robbery. While riding together with his friend Jeffrey White and Youngworth, Rossetti gang member John J. Jozapaitis pulled out a gun and shot White in the head, killing him. White's sin—that he knew too much about the Manchester truck robbery, had to die because he was weak and that this was a good opportunity to do it.

Although that murder had taken place nine years before, it left Youngworth scared and suspicious of both those in the criminal world and those in law enforcement.

So, ever cantankerous, Youngworth balked at telling the FBI what he knew about the Gardner heist, saying he wouldn't trust the investigators until they demonstrated they were willing to grant him his list of demands.

Still, the FBI discovered the location of the Brooklyn warehouse where the viewing of the purported Rembrandt masterpiece had taken place and raided it several months later. They found nothing in the unit Mashberg described, nor anywhere else in the storage facility.

With the heat getting more intense, Youngworth hired veteran criminal lawyer Martin Leppo to handle the negotiations with federal officials. But every time Leppo gained a concession, Youngworth would balk and instead rail that he was being set up. Finally, out of frustration with Youngworth, US attorney Donald Stern announced that he wouldn't engage in further talks with Youngworth, or anyone else for that matter, unless they brought forward hard evidence of access to the paintings.

"We have not yet been provided the kind of concrete and credible evidence one looks for in this case," Stern told reporters. "With all due respect, it's not credible and concrete just because I read it in the newspaper." Nonetheless, at one point in the fall of 1997, federal officials flew Connor to Massachusetts so he could meet with Youngworth in a room separated by a glass partition. Under law, Youngworth could not visit Connor in prison because Youngworth was also a convicted felon.

"There have been no negotiations—and there won't be—about what law enforcement might or might not be willing to do until there's some showing that we know what we're dealing with," Stern went on. "We want to have some confidence that what we're dealing with are priceless works of art—not the work of a bull artist."

Challenged to step up, Youngworth soon gave Mashberg a vial containing numerous small paint chips for delivery to the FBI. Youngworth contended that the chips came from *The Storm on the Sea of Galilee.* He also delivered twenty-five color photographs purportedly of the painting and the second Rembrandt stolen in the heist, *Lady and Gentleman in Black.* The verdict came less than a month later in separate public statements from the museum and federal investigators. The chips had not come from either of the two Rembrandts, and the photographs were not what Youngworth claimed they were, read a statement from Stern and Barry Mawn, head of the FBI's Boston office.

"We have conclusively determined that the paint chips were not authentic," the museum said.

However, neither statement mentioned another interesting finding of these tests: that the pigmentation and layering of the chips indicated that they had come from a seventeenth-century painting, the time period during which Rembrandt had worked. These tests were confirmed again recently by leading experts who said they could not rule out the possibility that the chips came from the stolen Vermeer, a contemporary of Rembrandt.

Of course, considering that he had operated an antiques store in Allston, Massachusetts, it could have been relatively easy for Youngworth to get his hands on paint chips of the right vintage. What's less clear is how he would have been able to get ahold of such a good replica of *The Storm on the Sea of Galilee* that it could have led a veteran reporter such as Mashberg to believe it was the real thing, if in fact it wasn't. Replicas of paintings can be obtained, but considering that the two men had met just a few weeks before the viewing, it is difficult to imagine that Youngworth could have arranged to have such a replica produced in such a short time.

But Anthony Amore, the Gardner's director of security, believes what Mashberg saw was a fake.

"Based on what I've learned about the structure of *The Storm,* and its well-varnished canvas, however, I lean toward it's not being the Gardner's painting," Amore wrote in the introduction to a book he co-authored with Mashberg about stolen Rembrandts.

The canvas of *The Storm* had been coated with varnish and lacquer often during its existence, so the idea that it could have been rolled up in any way, much less placed into a cylindrical tube and then removed from the storage unit as Mashberg reported, seemed almost impossible to him.

Mashberg, now a freelance journalist for the *New York Times* and other publications, has a mixed response. "Given how much I respect Anthony's opinion, I have to think now that it was a replica. But given the tests showing that the chips did come from Rembrandt's era, and the fact that I was on the same trail as the FBI seventeen years ago, I still think that the stolen paintings were in play in 1997."

As for Youngworth, while it is difficult to have sympathy for anyone who exaggerates and dissembles as much as he did, he too can be seen as a victim in this story. After his repeated attempts to persuade the authorities that he had the paintings failed, and left without anything to bargain away with the prosecution, he stood trial and was convicted of possessing a stolen vehicle. During his subsequent yearlong prison sentence, his wife, Judith, died of a drug overdose.

Still, Youngworth, who now lives modestly with his son in western Massachusetts, knows all too well the financial lure of the recovery of the stolen Gardner masterpieces. In 2001, he worked with his brother-in-law to produce copies of the stamp-size, self-portrait sketch of Rembrandt that had been among the pieces stolen from the museum.

A Rhode Island businessman facing federal prosecution for tax fraud whom Youngworth subsequently approached believed he could get authorities to postpone charging him if he could convince them he was working on recovering the Gardner paintings. In a late-night meeting in the parking lot of a Springfield restaurant, the businessman paid Youngworth $250,000 in cash for the sketch. But it was soon determined to be a forgery and the businessman was convicted of the tax evasion charges and sentenced. His claims that Youngworth had defrauded him of $250,000 were never pursued.

If Mashberg did see the Rembrandt in that warehouse in Brooklyn, he remains the only reporter to see any of the stolen pieces since the 1990 heist.

CHAPTER FOUR

ANNE HAWLEY'S BURDEN

F<small>ROM THE FIRST MOMENT</small> that spring morning in April 1994 that she opened the envelope containing a typewritten letter rather than the typical scrawled note, Gardner Museum director Anne Hawley knew what she had in her hands was something different. Though unsigned, the two-page letter was written with a command of legal terms, as if it had come from a lawyer, and conveyed a knowledge of the Gardner theft that only museum insiders and the FBI knew at the time.

The line "the perpetrators were not dressed as police officers, as reported by the press, but were dressed as security guards" immediately caught her attention.

"I have been asked to participate in a rather touchy issue that is of prime importance to your facility," the letter went on authoritatively. "The issue is the safe return of the missing art treasures." The thirteen pieces were all still together, the note said, and, most comforting for Hawley, who had worried constantly that they were not being well cared for, they were "stored in archival conditions to preserve them."

The letter touched off a frenzied two-week pursuit to commence negotiations for returning the artwork, and for Hawley at least, represents the most hopeful time of the twenty-five years she has spent trying to recover them. For a few weeks in 1994, she believed the nightmare of the Gardner heist might soon be over.

Hawley, who had been on the job only six months when the heist took place 1990, has weathered the frustrations of the investigation longer and perhaps more deeply than anyone else in Boston. While the federal investigation has involved the best efforts of five US attorneys, more than a dozen chiefs of the Boston FBI office, and three special agents in charge of the probe, the one person who has suffered the loss most is surely Anne Hawley.

For the then-forty-six-year-old Hawley, who had sought the position in the hope of restoring the Gardner to its turn-of-the-century brilliance, and who had neither the inclination nor the ability to solve crimes, she soon added that most high-profile responsibility to the long list of duties her job entailed.

Hawley had been told almost immediately after the heist that, in such high-end cases, if an arrest and recovery isn't made in the first few days, it was normal for years to pass before safe return of the missing artwork could be negotiated. But now, four years after the theft, hope of a safe return was exactly what she had in front of her.

The letter writer stated that the paintings had been stolen to gain someone a reduction in a prison sentence, but as that opportunity had dwindled dramatically there was no longer a primary motive for keeping the artwork. The best option for everyone involved, the letter said, was to negotiate a return of the pieces to the museum.

"All parties do want a resolution to everyone's satisfaction," Hawley read expectantly. "You get the collection and they get the money and immunity from prosecution." The writer stated that he did not know the identity of the men who had stolen the artwork, but instead was dealing with a third person who had approached him to carry out the negotiations.

Also, to underscore the importance of taking him seriously and dealing with him immediately, the writer stated that the artwork was currently held in a "non–common law country." As such, if any of the pieces were sold to someone, likely for a significant price, that buyer might have a legitimate claim that he or she now owned the piece, regardless of the fact that someone else had stolen it from the museum.

And, the writer went on, two key factors needed to be dealt with before any return could be gained: First, a ransom amount had to be agreed on, and second, the representative and his clients had to be assured that the FBI would not seek to arrest them during negotiations.

There would be no bargaining over how much he wanted the museum to give him for safe return of the paintings, either. In total, the writer estimated the value of the artwork to be $260 million. He wanted $2.6 million for their return. The $2.6 million would be sent to a designated offshore bank account at the same time the artwork was handed over, the letter stated.

Not unreasonable, Hawley thought as she read the terms. While at the time the museum had posted a reward of $1 million for the paintings' return, it would soon up the ante to $5 million, the largest announced reward for the return of any masterpiece.

But negotiating their return without involving law enforcement would of course be far trickier. With that in mind he proposed a unique idea: To show him that the museum was interested in negotiating, it should ask the *Boston Globe* to include the numeral one in front of the decimal point for the value of the dollar against the Italian lira in the currency column it ran inside the Sunday business pages.

Hawley finished reading and was astonished and excited. The letter had the right mix of authority and caution for her to be convinced it was real. That morning, after more than four years of dealing with fraud artists and fakers who claimed they could facilitate the return of the artwork only to have her hopes dashed, Hawley felt she was finally dealing with someone who had something.

She quickly referred the letter to the FBI's Boston office, who immediately contacted *Globe* editor Matthew V. Storin, asking if the paper would be willing to go along with the plan outlined in the letter.

"I saw it as a community-service decision," Storin said later. He was unwilling to list an inaccurate value for the lira, but Storin said he would add a numeral one prominently in the exchange rate listings. First, though, he extracted an agreement from Richard S. Swensen, the FBI's agent in charge of the Boston office, to pledge to tell the *Globe* first if its efforts led to the recovery of the paintings.

Swensen agreed, and the following Sunday, May 1, 1994, the numeral one appeared in the middle of the row that listed the official exchange rate for the Italian lira. Several days later a second letter, this one postmarked May 3, 1994, was in Hawley's morning mail. Like the earlier one, it looked as though it had been written on an electric typewriter and it was unsigned.

The letter began on a hopeful note: The placement of the numeral inside the currency box showed the writer the museum was interested in negotiating.

But then the bad news:

"I am also fully aware of the massive alert that the federal, state and Boston authorities went on last Friday afternoon" seeking to make an arrest while the negotiations commenced.

The $ abroad

Selected foreign currency values in US dollars.

Australian dollar		$0.7120
British pound		$1.5200
Canadian dollar		$0.7225
French franc		$0.1771
German mark		$0.6072
Hong Kong dollar		$0.1295
Irish punt		$1.4759
Israeli shekel		$0.3336
Italian lira	1	$0.000627
Japanese yen		$0.009935
Mexican peso		$0.306466
Dutch guilder		$0.5407
Spanish peseta		$0.007438
Swedish krona		$0.1309
Swiss franc		$0.7156

Prices Friday, from Globe wire services. Rates are commnercial.

At the urging of the FBI and Gardner director Anne Hawley, the *Globe* agreed to drop the numeral I into the middle of the currency box that ran in its Sunday Business section, May 1, 1994, showing an anonymous letter-writer that the museum was willing to enter into secret negotiations for the return of the stolen artwork.

"I think it important to say right now that you have a choice, that is you may be able to apprehend a low-level participant who has been kept in the dark or you can recapture the entire collection intact. YOU CANNOT HAVE BOTH."

Hawley was dumbfounded. She had impressed on Swensen and others at the FBI her hope that the letter writer was legitimate and that everyone needed to follow his instructions to the letter. That word had filtered down to the handful of agents who were directly responsible for the case.

"We were told to stand down by Swensen, and that's exactly what we did. No calls were made, no one was interviewed," says one agent working the case at the time.

However, he said, that word may not have reached everyone inside the Bureau. Agents in the Boston and New York offices were working feverishly to track down the letter writer's identity, the agent said.

"There was no complete stand-down," the agent admitted. "Far from it."

As a result, the letter writer said he needed time to evaluate his options. While those who held the stolen artwork needed money and might be willing to reconnect with the museum, he was worried.

"The onerous penalties related to this venture make me extremely wary of everything," he wrote.

If he decided it was impossible to continue negotiating, he would provide the museum with "a few solid clues where you can apply pressure to get the collection."

But no clues were forthcoming. Hawley never heard from him again after that.

"I was heartbroken with how it turned out," Hawley remembered even a decade later, the sting still in her voice. "Finally, I felt I was dealing with someone who knew something, who could get us somewhere, and just as quickly it disappeared. It was heartbreaking, really."

ALTHOUGH IT MAY HAVE BEEN the biggest disappointment, and the closest Hawley feels the museum has yet come to recovering the stolen art, the episode with the anonymous letters was not the only time she became emotionally involved in the investigation only to be let down in the end. In fact, she and trustee

Arnold Hiatt even met in a New York hotel room with William Youngworth, the ex-convict who had driven Tom Mashberg to a deserted warehouse, and who on more than one occasion raised expectations that he could facilitate the return of the paintings. Like Hawley, Hiatt was convinced that Youngworth could be trusted, and gave him $10,000 to advance his efforts.

She also pleaded with then-senator Edward M. Kennedy, the state's most powerful politician, to spur the FBI in its investigation, and suggested to William Bulger, president of the State Senate and a personal friend, that he ask his brother, James "Whitey" Bulger, the notorious Boston gangster arrested by the FBI in 2011 after years of eluding them, if he knew who might have pulled off the heist.

And after years of frustration, Hawley had a surprising bit of inspiration: If the FBI couldn't succeed in getting her paintings back, she reasoned that maybe the pope could help. So in 1999 the museum reached out to Bishop William F. Murphy, head of the Catholic diocese on Long Island, in the hope of convincing Pope John Paul II to issue a papal appeal for the paintings' return. Particular mention was made that one of the works was Rembrandt's seascape portraying Christ calming his disciples as their boat made its way through a storm-tossed Sea of Galilee.

The pope never stepped in, however. Vatican officials said such intervention would lead to other unconventional requests.

One option Hawley hasn't tried is using the Internet and social media to maximize awareness of the specific pieces that are missing and encouraging the public's involvement in the search. Crowdsourcing—in this case, reaching out to the public in helping solve crimes—has even been credited in at least two major manhunts in Boston recently.

This strategy famously brought Whitey Bulger to justice in 2011, after the FBI made a public appeal that focused on Catherine Greig, Bulger's girlfriend. Greig was recognized by a neighbor near the couple's Santa Monica, California, hideout, who phoned in a tip.

Having the public's assistance with an investigation was also instrumental in the arrest of one of the so-called Boston Marathon bombers, Dzhokhar Tsarnaev, in April 2013. Less than an hour after releasing Watertown residents from a full-day lockdown following an overnight shooting that killed one of the two brothers allegedly involved in the bombing, a resident found a trail of blood that led to Tsarnaev, hiding beneath the tarp covering the pleasure boat parked in his backyard.

Still, the museum has not pressed government, business, or community leaders to issue public appeals for assistance in the Gardner case.

"They have to be somewhere" is a common refrain investigators hear about the missing paintings. Many members of the public, particularly in neighborhoods with a lot of criminal activity, where the artwork might thus be stashed, likely are wary of dealing with the FBI or law enforcement in general. Yet it surely would be easier to gain their trust through appeals by people they know, such as community leaders or even celebrities.

The effectiveness of such campaigns recently has been seen more and more, digital marketing and research companies have found. Well-run initiatives have been able to tap the power of people: from the mapping of a gold mine in Ontario, Canada, that led to the discovery of 8 million ounces of gold to offering unique ideas to improve public education.

"The concept of using social media tools to leverage the people and networks connected to Boston to uncover the secrets of the Gardner heist and the missing masterpieces is a no-brainer," says John Della Volpe, CEO of SocialSphere, a digital marketing and research company in Cambridge. "Worst case, the world learns about Rembrandt's only seascape, best case some of the world's most valuable art is returned to its rightful owners, the community of Boston."

Pierre Tabel, former head of the art theft unit established by the French national police, says his unit benefited greatly from the public's assistance and support in their efforts to recover stolen paintings. The 1985 theft of nine Impressionist paintings from the Marmottan Monet Museum in Paris was considered a "national disgrace" for France. Spurred by the public's outrage, his superiors were constantly urging him to waste no resources to recover the paintings, which were returned in 1990.

But such an outcry for public assistance has been largely absent from the pursuit of the Gardner paintings. Hawley has mourned alone what the loss of the artwork has meant to Boston and the public at large.

"The theft of these rare and important treasures of art is a tragic loss to the art world and to society as a whole," Hawley said in a 2008 statement. "Imagine never being able to hear a performance of Beethoven's Fifth, read Herman Melville's *Moby Dick*, or listen to a Louis Armstrong jazz piece ever again. . . . The loss of these remarkable masterpieces removes a part of our culture essential to our society."

WHETHER OUT OF DESPERATION or frustration or both, not all of Hawley's ideas for recovering the Gardner masterpieces have been well thought through.

In 2005, Hawley directed the museum to hire a British private investigator who had earned enormous success in tracking art theft. She was so impressed with the work that Jurek Rokoszynski, a former officer with London's metropolitan police force, had done in recovering two multimillion-dollar paintings by nineteenth-century British landscape artist J. M. W. Turner stolen from an exhibit by the Tate Gallery of London that she convinced the museum to pay him almost $150,000 to help recover the Gardner pieces.

Hawley hoped that Rokoszynski would somehow be able to infiltrate Boston's underworld and find a connection who might lead him to the Gardner paintings. The problem was that while Rokoszynski (or "Rocky," as everyone called him) was built like a man of steel and had the bravado to match, he had little of the needed wiles to convince anyone that he was a criminal. His heavy British accent, moreover, likely raised questions among Boston's Irish toughs.

So instead Rocky spent his time reading about the case, either in newspaper files or court records. Then he was introduced to John "Joey" Nichols, a youthful house thief who was about to be released from county jail and had written to the museum saying he knew what had happened to the stolen paintings.

"My parents knew someone, a former owner of a gallery in Boston who lives in Florida now," Nichols told Rokoszynski. "He collects all sorts of art and he wound up with the paintings."

Although skeptical at the outset, Rocky grew more intrigued when Nichols told him that his father knew Frank "Cadillac Frank" Salemme, a major organized crime figure in Boston, and had hung out with Carmello Merlino, whose Dorchester auto body garage was being investigated for possible ties to the museum heist. As a clincher, Nichols passed on to Rocky the name of the Boston gallery owner his father believed had possession of the paintings, Charles G. Martignette.

Martignette was known in the art world, but not for the Great Masters whose works were featured on the Gardner's walls. Instead, he specialized in pin-up art, the risqué illustrations featured in numerous magazines catering to men in the decades before *Playboy* and *Penthouse* came into existence. An acknowledged authority in the field of American illustration art and internationally recognized as an author, dealer, appraiser, and collector of original artwork by America's great twentieth-century illustrators and artists, Martignette counted in his collection more than 10,000 works, the largest in the world. He co-wrote *The Great American Pin-up*, which, with 900 illustrations, was considered the bible of the genre.

Nichols was convinced that Martignette had gotten ahold of the stolen Gardner paintings through connections in the underworld and that he had been able to transport them to Belize, where he was planning to open an art gallery.

After months delaying Rocky from meeting with Martignette, Nichols settled on a plan: the two would fly on Rocky's tab to southern Florida to approach Martignette at his condominium in Hallandale. Nichols told Rocky that he had called Martignette beforehand and told him they were coming. He also told Martignette that Rocky had something to do with artwork, but not that he was from the Gardner Museum and on the hunt for the stolen paintings.

Once the pair arrived at a hotel a few miles from Martignette's home, Nichols delayed the meeting several more days. Rocky, impatient at best, began to fume at Nichols, who all the while drove up the hotel bill the museum was paying for with full dinners in the dining room and late-night drinking bouts at the bar. Finally, three days after arriving at the hotel, Rocky said he'd had enough.

"If you don't take me to see Martignette tomorrow, I'm going on my own," Rocky told him.

"That won't get you anywhere," Nichols told him bluntly. "The only way you'll get him to cooperate is if you let me talk to him first."

The next morning the two men drove to Martignette's gated complex, arguing all the way over how the approach would take place.

"We'll go in together," Rocky told Nichols. "You'll introduce me as from the Gardner Museum, and I'll take it from there. This has gone on long enough."

"No," Nichols insisted. "Let me go in first. I'll tell him you're in the car and want to come in and talk to him."

Martignette seemed surprised to see Nichols when he knocked on the door. Nichols explained that he was working with the Gardner Museum on recovering their stolen masterpieces. It was just registering what was going on when Rocky came bursting through the door, shouting at Martignette.

"Okay, I know you know where our paintings are," Rocky yelled. "Start talking now!"

Rocky was enormous. Martignette knew immediately he wasn't going to listen to anything he said, so he retreated and called the police.

Hallandale police captain Kenneth Cowley was one of the first officers to arrive on the scene. He found Martignette and Rocky shouting at each other at the top of their lungs. "I'm not too sure either knew what the other was saying," Cowley remembered later. "The big guy had a pretty good British accent, but I did hear him shouting about getting his museum's paintings back. But it was Mr. Martignette's apartment, so I ordered the big fellow to leave, and we would straighten it out at the police station."

A few days later, Cowley thought he had it sorted out after interviewing Martignette, Nichols, and Rocky.

"Nichols was telling the museum's investigator something that he had no evidence of: that Martignette had something to do with these stolen paintings and that they had gotten somehow to Belize."

But Cowley said that Rocky refused to give up on his suspicions about Martignette, and intimated that he was going to try to interview Martignette again on his own.

"That was it for me," Cowley said. "I told him that he was no longer welcome in Hallandale, and if he didn't leave immediately, I would be calling his employer."

According to public documents, Rocky was paid about $150,000 by the museum for the eighteen months in 2005 and 2006 he spent trying to track the stolen artwork. Following his return to England, he assisted in making a documentary about better times: his work recovering the Turner masterpieces for the Tate Gallery.

YEARS OF FRUSTRATING RECOVERY EFFORTS like the disappointments involving Nichols and Youngworth wore heavy on Hawley, and she gave up her lead role on behalf of the Gardner in pursuing the stolen paintings. In 2005, she hired Anthony Amore, a former US Transportation Security Administration agent, to maintain security at the museum while working closely with the FBI on its investigation.

Smart and indefatigable, Amore was able to develop a productive working relationship with the FBI and the US attorney's office, allowing him to work alongside agents and investigators on the tips that came in, while steeping himself in the leads that had not worked out in the years before he began working the case.

He also built a private database, including the details of hundreds of art thefts dating back to the early 1900s, in hopes it would provide clues to better understanding what happened in the Gardner theft. He combed old files, libraries, and books about thefts for such clues as what time of day the theft took place, whether the thieves used force or trickery to gain entry, whether a weapon was used, whether the thieves had an inside connection, how many pieces were stolen, how long it took for the thieves to surface, and when they did, whether they revealed themselves to the museum itself or to an intermediary.

After years of legwork, Amore came to agree with Richard DesLauriers, chief of the FBI's Boston office, that the stolen artwork had found its way into the possession of Robert Guarente, a Boston hood who resided in Maine, and that after Guarente developed cancer in 2001, he turned over at least three of the pieces to his friend Robert Gentile of Manchester, Connecticut.

In 2010, Amore and FBI agent Geoff Kelly were the first investigators to interview Guarente's widow, who told them her husband had passed the stolen artwork to Gentile in the parking lot of a Portland, Maine, restaurant. Amore advanced Mrs. Guarente $1,000 from the museum to have her car fixed, the reason she'd decided to contact them about what she knew. Amore was also with Gentile in his prison cell following a search of his home, pleading with him to share what had happened to the paintings that investigators were sure Gentile had stashed away.

Gentile stonewalled: He maintained he knew nothing of the heist.

Amore appears to take such frustrating twists in stride, and he says he remains hopeful that a recovery will take place before too long. Even when a lead doesn't develop, Amore sees the bright side: "It's one less haystack we have to search to find the needle."

With Kelly in the lead, Amore has participated in FBI searches of residences in Maine, New Hampshire, and Massachusetts in search of the missing artwork. To this day, Amore says he speaks to Kelly daily about leads each is working on, and they often conduct interviews related to those leads together.

Amore appeared with Kelly at a March 2013 press conference in which DesLauriers, then still head of the FBI's Boston office, made the dramatic announcement that they believed they knew not only who had carried out the theft but that there had been attempts to fence the artwork in Philadelphia a decade before.

Although his remarks were not as dramatic as DesLauriers', Amore said in a radio interview not long after the press conference that they indeed had made progress in solving the case. But within a month, Amore was failing to return phone calls from reporters seeking information about whether the bombshell announcement had produced new leads.

However, the lack of any significant developments hasn't stopped Amore from making public appearances to talk about the Gardner case and, even more so, to sell the book he co-wrote in 2011. Titled *Stealing Rembrandts: The Untold Stories of Notorious Art Heists*, it discusses several thefts of Rembrandts from individual museums and galleries over the years, but gives scant mention of the theft that Amore—and the world—is most intrigued by: the 1990 Gardner heist.

The brief mention the book gives to the Gardner case focuses on the alleged viewing of Rembrandt's seascape by Amore's co-author, Tom Mashberg, and blames the failure of leading to a recovery to the animosity between Mashberg's source, Youngworth, and federal investigators—not to the substance of Youngworth's information.

ALTHOUGH IT TOOK PLACE IN BOSTON and Governor Michael S. Dukakis was a close friend of the museum's director, neither the Massachusetts state police nor the Boston police department was involved in the investigation after the preliminary review of the crime scene. Instead, the investigation has been controlled by the FBI and involved only a handful of special agents and their supervisors. But believing that the thieves would be taking the stolen artwork across state lines, the FBI asserted its jurisdiction over the case.

In the early going, the manpower was much greater. Within days of the heist, more than forty agents were assigned to the case, following up dozens of leads. One of the first that caused a scramble inside the museum was a bomb threat, apparently called in by a gang looking to get the FBI's attention. "We also are being threatened from the outside by criminals who want attention from the FBI, and so they were threatening us, and threatening putting bombs in the museum," Anne Hawley said recently. "We were evacuating the museum, the staff members were under threat, no one really knew what kind of a conundrum we were in."

Investigators needed to follow up on every lead, regardless how farfetched it appeared. One of the first leads the agents appeared to take seriously involved museum employees. The agents asked for the names of all older Italian women who worked stitching the tapestry and pieces of cloth at the museum, after a tip that a Boston gang member was related to one of them. The list was prepared but no connection was ever determined.

Two Boston cops assigned to the US attorney's office on organized crime investigations also were convinced they knew who had pulled off the theft. They had received a tip from a reliable contact that John L. Sullivan Jr., a South Boston amateur artist as well as a petty thief, had been seen around the Gardner Museum in the days leading up to the theft, and confirmed it through parking tickets.

But again, the jurisdiction belonged to the FBI, and entreaties to the agents to follow up on the tip fell on deaf ears, with one agent telling them "we've got dozens of suspects that we've got to chase down."

Within three months, the number of agents assigned to the case had been drastically reduced. In fact, it went down to just one—Daniel Falzon, a young agent from San Francisco, where his father was a police officer. Boston was his first permanent assignment and the Gardner heist, understandably, was the biggest case he ever spearheaded. Although he could call for assistance from other agents, he did most of the legwork and all the decision-making on the myriad tips the FBI received.

By the time he got the case, Falzon was already familiar with Myles Connor Jr., the one person whose name would forever be associated with art theft in the Boston area.

According to Connor, he had long cased the Gardner Museum, and as it turned out, it may have been Falzon's investigative work on another case that was responsible for Connor being behind bars when it did take place. In 1988, two years before the Gardner theft, Falzon received a tip that Connor was trying to fence two antique dueling pistols that were believed stolen.

Falzon sent a lengthy confidential report on his probe to other FBI offices nationally, and it drew the interest of an agent in Springfield, Illinois, who was investigating Connor for trying to sell everything from cocaine and LSD to stolen antiques and paintings. An undercover buy was arranged, and Connor was charged with trying to sell a Simon Willard grandfather clock that had been stolen from the Woolworth Estate in Monmouth in 1974, and two paintings worth $300,000 that had been stolen in 1975 from the Mead Art Museum at Amherst College. In November 1989, four months before the Gardner theft, Connor pleaded guilty to the criminal charges and was sentenced to twenty years in federal prison.

It wasn't just the good guys who were looking for the thieves. According to a past associate, notorious Boston gangster Whitey Bulger asked him to find out who might have pulled off the crime of the century. Being located in the Fens neighborhood of Boston, the museum was considered part of Bulger's turf, and whoever was responsible for such a heist would have to pay a tribute, a percentage of the value of what was taken, to Bulger or be threatened—or worse—until they did.

Bulger associate Kevin Weeks told me that he came up with several names, including Sullivan's, the South Boston amateur artist, as possibly involved, but got no further. Bulger also told Stephen "Rifleman" Flemmi, his second in command, to find out who was responsible, but Flemmi too came back empty-handed, except for a rumor that the paintings had been flown out of the country, possibly to Saudi Arabia, the day after the robbery.

Then, working on the belief that most museum heists have an insider as an active participant, the FBI administered lie detector tests to both night watchmen working the night of the theft. Randy Hestand, who had been called in to work in place of the regular man on duty, passed without a flaw. Rick Abath failed at least one of the questions and was ordered to take it a second time. Abath claims he failed the first test only because the FBI asked him about recreational drug use, and that he passed the second test.

The natural air of suspicion that surrounds any case involving the FBI was even more pronounced in the Gardner case. Agents were not sharing information with anyone inside the museum, including Lyle Grindle, then director of museum security. And when they asked Grindle or anyone else at the museum for information, they provided no explanation as to why it was relevant to the investigation.

It took more than a month for the FBI to send for an analyst who knew how to examine the computer that contained the case's key forensic evidence—the path the thieves had taken during their eighty-eight minutes inside the museum's galleries. Even then no one bothered to interview the technicians who had been installing the museum's security system for the prior two years.

The museum's trustees also felt they were being kept in the dark about the status of the investigation. Trustee Francis W. Hatch, Jr. recalled one meeting held ostensibly to gain a briefing from the agent and supervisor on the case. "They wouldn't tell us anything about what they thought of the robbery or who they considered suspects," Hatch recalls. "It was very embarrassing to all of us."

Then, while in England to attend a wedding, Hatch decided to look up Richard Ellis, head of the art theft squad for the New Scotland Yard, who had just recovered masterpieces stolen from an English mansion. Ellis had studied the Gardner theft in enough depth to give Hatch more information about the possible suspects than Hatch had received from the FBI.

Ellis told Hatch he believed the job had been pulled off by local toughs, not professional art thieves, and that it might take years but that the artwork would be returned when the thieves or their fence needed a favor from federal prosecutors.

"I was so impressed with him—he had great bearing, and he talked openly and confidently—and optimistically about what to expect," Hatch says. "It was a whole lot different than how the FBI was treating us."

Hatch convinced the trustees that the museum needed to hire a firm to investigate, and stay in touch with the FBI on its probe. IGI, a private investigative firm based in Washington begun by Terry Lenzner, who had cut his teeth as a lawyer for the Senate Watergate Committee, was put on retainer, and the executive assigned to the case was Larry Potts, a former top deputy in the FBI.

Fearful that their authority was being undercut, the FBI's supervisors in Boston complained to US attorney Wayne Budd, who fired off a memo warning the museum that it faced prosecution if it withheld information relevant to the investigation. Hatch responded, saying in his letter that he was "shocked and saddened" by Budd's attempt to "intimidate" the museum and that it cast "a pall over future cooperative efforts."

Similarly, convincing the FBI to share its responsibilities on the case with the Boston police department and the Massachusetts state police was apparently an impossible proposition. The FBI asked Boston detectives Francis J. McCarthy and Carl Washington, who conducted the initial investigation, to file their reports and then never consulted the two again. Ray Flynn, then Boston's mayor, says he remains baffled as to why the FBI never sought the assistance of Boston police.

"The Gardner art theft in Boston was devastating," Flynn recalled recently. "Boston police were pretty much taken off the scene of the investigation by the feds, and we never could quite understand why that was the policy. Our robbery squad knew every wise guy in the city and had some reliable informants. They grew up and lived in Boston. Why wouldn't they hear things during an investigation?"

But the FBI resisted such a move from the outset. One agent, knowing Flynn's hunch to be true, told his superiors it would be a good idea to use the investigative resources of the Boston and state police and recommended a joint task force, if not an informal one. He was told bluntly that neither department had sufficient people to lend to the investigation, and a cooperative agreement was never signed.

Traditionally the FBI has resisted seeking assistance from local law enforcement in investigating federal crimes, out of concern that confidential information might fall into the wrong hands and become known by the press or, even worse, those under investigation. Others in law enforcement, however, say the reason is that the FBI doesn't like sharing the decision-making on major cases—or the federal funds that go into the cases. And of course there's the public approval—the glory—that comes with solving major crimes.

Thomas J. Foley, who joined the state police in 1984 and rose through the ranks to head the department, says his department was never asked to join the Gardner investigation.

"We would have jumped on it, but the Bureau has this pride about doing things their way," says Foley, who co-wrote a book highly critical of the FBI's pursuit of Whitey Bulger.

"The FBI is not about sharing any glory with the state cops, no less Boston," Foley says. "Of course, that means they didn't have the advantage of our sources or our expertise. I think we could have helped, but no one ever asked for it."

Then-governor Dukakis says he stood ready to lend the assistance of the Massachusetts state police to the investigation, especially since he felt kinship with the museum, having been taken to it often as a child by his mother, and being a personal friend of Anne Hawley. But the call for assistance never came.

"The place is so wonderful now that we tend to forget what a horrendous thing it was to have happened," Dukakis recalled recently. "The wearing of police uniforms always bothered me, and then the seeming difficulty of being able to identify them."

Hawley too, he said, has shared with him and his wife, Kitty, a very close friend, her frustration that the FBI has been unable to recover any of the stolen pieces.

"She's frustrated, highly skeptical about a lot of the stuff," he said. "She's gotten tired with everything. Enough already."

The FBI claims to understand that frustration, but has no plans to alter its investigative strategy on the case: check out every lead that comes in, and stress publicly that no one will be prosecuted if they show up with the stolen pieces but instead will be eligible for the $5 million reward the museum has offered for their return.

Three successive US attorneys have publicly announced that anyone facilitating the return of the stolen artwork would not be prosecuted. But those announcements, which have been widely reported by the media, have not prompted a breakthrough lead. In fact, Falzon and Kelly, two of the three FBI agents who have been the lead investigators on the case for years, have stated that they have never received a concrete lead.

"In the last twenty years, and the last eight that I've had the case, there hasn't been a concrete sighting, or real 'proof of life,'" Kelly stated in 2010 on the occasion of the twentieth anniversary of the theft. "At the same time I can't get discouraged about it. It would be very difficult to put my heart in this investigation if I allowed myself to get discouraged." More recently, Kelly told a TV reporter that the FBI had received a "confirmed sighting" of one of the pieces, but did not provide any details of the sighting or identify the individual who had made the claim.

All investigative techniques have been used: throwing witnesses in front of federal grand juries; undercover operations; DNA testing of and trying to lift fingerprints from crime scene evidence; house searches; threatening reluctant witnesses with prosecution on minor crimes; and, in the case of Robert Gentile, actually going through with prosecution.

The FBI has even utilized psychics to help in the investigation, including the seer who in 1982 helped locate a US Army brigadier general who had been taken hostage and hidden by Italian extremists.

The one significant approach the FBI has not tried is expanding the investigation with fresh eyes and resources—sharing the probe with a task force of other federal and local police agencies.

If there had been such involvement at the outset of the probe, the FBI might have been aware from the earliest days after the theft that the Massachusetts state police were already investigating the criminal network headed by Carmello Merlino and Robert Guarente on a cocaine trafficking scheme. The state police probe included surveillance of figures the FBI would later view as major suspects in the theft, before and after the Gardner heist took place.

An expanded investigation might also have brought to the FBI's attention, long before they began focusing on him, claims that Bobby Guarente wound up with the paintings.

In 2005, Guarente's daughter and his best friend spoke to a Boston lawyer about the possibility that Guarente had kept several of the masterpieces stashed in his farmhouse in Madison, Maine. But FBI agents didn't begin focusing on Guarente until 2010, when his widow, looking for cash, summoned them to tell what she knew of her late husband's possession of the paintings.

FBI agent Kelly says that while he appreciates that state and local police have been ready to assist in the investigation whenever the FBI has sought their help, he believes that opening the probe to a task force would be counterproductive.

"I don't think a task force per se [would be productive]," Kelly insisted in 2010. "As years go on, there's fewer and fewer people who have a good knowledge of the case. It would just take too long to get everyone up to speed."

That position was echoed by the head of the FBI a year later, after then-senator John F. Kerry wrote to FBI director Robert S. Mueller asking what assistance the FBI might need to spur the investigation.

"Thanks for the interest but our current manpower and structure is fine," Mueller responded. "If a lead develops that requires more hands, the Boston office can call on the resources of the FBI's Art Theft Squad to assist it."

Yet the FBI agents who control the Gardner case can treat even a member of the FBI's own art theft squad as an outsider. Robert K. Wittman helped form the unit for the FBI in the 1990s and led several undercover operations that successfully recovered millions of dollars' worth of art that had been stolen from museums, private galleries, and homes.

In 2006, he received a tip that two Frenchmen with alleged ties to mobsters in Corsica were hinting that they could deliver the stolen Vermeer, valued at more than $100 million, and at least one of the two large Rembrandts that were taken. Working on the lead put Wittman in contact with the two agents who controlled the case for the FBI's Boston office, agent Kelly and his supervisor, whom Wittman identified only as "Fred."

For more than a year Wittman engaged the two intermediaries, working with Kelly and his supervisor, as well as French police, who also became convinced that the two mobsters had access to not only the stolen Gardner paintings but seventy other stolen pieces as well. But the operation fell apart, Wittman says, because of bureaucratic impediments imposed on him by Kelly's supervisor and, to a lesser degree, French authorities.

Wittman says Fred micromanaged Wittman's interactions with the two French accomplices, even though he was unfamiliar with overseeing an undercover operation. At one point, Wittman claims, Fred tried to get Wittman thrown off the case by sending an official memorandum to FBI chiefs in Washington questioning whether Wittman was trying to delay completing the investigation until retiring so he could win the $5 million reward as a private citizen.

In addition, Wittman says, Fred—who had never before traveled to a foreign country on official business—was quick to offend his French counterparts on a trip to France, seeking to assert the FBI's control of the case even though many of the dealings were to take place inside that country. Despite Wittman's pleas, FBI officials refused to wrest control of the investigation from this supervisor because of the historic reluctance of those at FBI headquarters to overrule the decisions of the agency's local supervisors.

Wittman described his frustrations investigating the lead, which he described as the best the FBI had gotten in the Gardner theft, in his 2010 autobiography *Priceless: How I Went Undercover to Rescue the World's Stolen Treasures.*

"Bureaucracies and turf fighting on both sides of the Atlantic had destroyed the best chance in a decade to rescue the Gardner paintings," Wittman wrote. "We'd blown an opportunity to infiltrate a major art crime ring in France, a loose network of mobsters holding as many as 70 stolen masterpieces."

More recently, Wittman stood behind his criticisms voiced against the FBI's tradition of tightly guarding its investigations and refusing to share control or information with local agencies.

"If anything, I've gotten more convinced that the Bureau needs to open up with other federal agencies as well as local and state law enforcement," Wittman says. "To close itself off to the intelligence, expertise, and resources that exist elsewhere just to be in control of the investigation makes no sense, whether you're talking about the Gardner case or any other one that has been as drawn-out and complicated as it has."

PART III
THE FEDS

CHAPTER FIVE

EIGHT ON A
SCALE OF TEN

O N THE ANNIVERSARY of the Gardner heist, typically, Anne
Hawley would release a statement underscoring what
the loss of the thirteen pieces meant to the art-loving public and, likewise, plead for their return and ask that whoever
might be holding the paintings keep them in dry, climate-
controlled surroundings. In other years, the FBI would mark
the anniversary of the theft without much more than a press
release or perhaps an interview with the special agent in
charge of the Boston office, emphasizing that the case was still
under investigation.

But this time was different. The day before the twenty-
third anniversary in 2013, the FBI called a press conference
to announce the progress it had made in its investigation of
the Gardner heist. In the days leading up to the event there
was a definite uncertainty among those of us who had been

following the case about what to expect. I made my usual calls, but no one seemed to know what day the event would be held, or even where. Some sources said it would take place at the FBI's office in downtown Boston; others said it would be at the museum itself.

Then a previously helpful investigator, with whom I had been sharing information on the case for what seemed like ages, suddenly distanced himself from me. When I heard that some of the brass within the FBI were considering having the press conference at FBI headquarters in Washington, DC, I tracked down my source and pressed him.

"On a scale of one to ten, what number would you give to the importance of what they're going to say tomorrow?" I asked him, almost desperate for any tidbit of information.

"Eight," he said flatly, then hung up.

He had plenty to compare it to. Long before the midnight theft at the Gardner Museum shocked the world, Massachusetts had seen more than its share of art heists. Undoubtedly, because of the unusually large number of museums, galleries, libraries, and private homes that were graced with rare beauties, or maybe because of the shockingly poor security in those places, police and federal agents had chased dozens of such thefts.

In the 1970s, only four years apart, Rembrandts were stolen on three occasions: twice from Boston's Museum of Fine Arts and once from the Worcester Art Museum. Six paintings, on loan from Harvard's Fogg Museum, were stolen from the home of Harvard president Derek Bok and his wife, noted author Sissela Bok, while they slept in 1976.

Three years before that, three Jackson Pollocks, valued at an estimated $1 million, were stolen from the Cambridge home of a Harvard professor. One of the Pollocks was recovered three years later when George S. Abrams, the lawyer for the professor, found similarities between the break-in at his client's home and a robbery nearby in which the robbers were caught. Spurred by the detective work of Abrams, himself a respected art collector, Cambridge district judge Arthur Sherman made a deal with the robbers: Return the Pollocks and get a more lenient sentence. One of the Pollocks suddenly showed up a short time later. (A second one showed up years later when the holder sought to get it officially authenticated as a Pollock, and the third remains missing to this day.)

Shortly thereafter, nine paintings, including works by Monticelli, Gainsborough, and Maxfield, were stolen from the Brockton home of the industrialist H. James Stone in May 1977. Then, less than a year after that, six masterpieces, including a Rembrandt, an El Greco, and a Bruegel, were stolen from a Cohasset residence. Remarkably, those last six were recovered the next year in an abandoned Dorchester parking lot after the owner refused to pay the ransom.

Despite the steady stream of thefts, these losses were treated with chilling nonchalance by law enforcement. As Daniel Golden reported in 1989 in the *Boston Globe Sunday Magazine*, only two police officers in the US investigated art thefts full-time: one in Los Angeles and the other in New York. The FBI, which is called in on all thefts of goods worth $50,000 or more, does not have a single agent concentrating solely on art. By contrast, Italy's art theft unit has eighty agents and has recovered 100,000 items since 1970.

"Very little police manpower is devoted to investigating art theft," Constance Lowenthal, director of the International Foundation for Art Research in New York City, told Golden at the time. "Police departments don't realize that it's different from stealing a television. You have to have a certain vocabulary and knowledge. [It]'s a billion-dollar problem getting very little attention."

Golden's article, ironically published about a year before the Gardner heist, carried a clear warning that museums, especially those the size of the Gardner, were in peril. The value of art in the 1980s hanging in galleries and homes around the US, but especially in well-to-do Boston, had skyrocketed, but law enforcement had shown little ability or inclination to protect the pieces.

Unfortunately for the Gardner Museum, things didn't really start to change until after they were so audaciously robbed. Museums of all sizes realized they too had been operating with inadequate security in place. People like Steven Keller, the Florida-based museum security specialist hired by the Gardner, found business booming, as museums rushed to install state-of-the-art equipment to improve their surveillance and alarm systems.

"No one would admit it, but there was a common sentiment amongst Boston's museum set after seeing what had happened at the Gardner Museum. 'There but for fortune . . . '" Keller now says, thinking of how vulnerable his clients were before they called him.

The capabilities, not to mention the interests, of law enforcement changed dramatically in the years after the Gardner theft. Lawmakers, too, got in on the act. Edward M. Kennedy, the senior senator from Massachusetts at the time of the heist, whose grandfather had been a personal friend of Isabella Gardner, offered museum director Anne Hawley his considerable political help after the theft. By 1994, he had offered an amendment to federal law, expanding the FBI's jurisdiction to prosecute theft of art and other cultural antiquities from museums, and increasing the maximum sentence convicted art thieves could face, from six to twenty years.

In turn, the FBI created an art theft squad, concentrating solely on the crimes. The seven agents currently assigned to that squad have participated in numerous undercover operations aimed at striking as such thefts are being planned and attacking the attendant fencing operations.

Perhaps if such a force had been in place in 1984, the squad—or a consultant working with them—would have taken more seriously the 1984 theft of four original paintings worth $40,000 from a gallery in Hingham, Massachusetts. On that occasion, the owner, Patricia Jobe Pierce, was beaten when she resisted two thieves who walked off with the paintings. Although Pierce was hospitalized as a result of the attack, and the local police investigated the theft as a legitimate one, the FBI considered the assault part of an elaborate fraud. Among the four stolen paintings was one by Edmund C. Tarbell that Pierce had bought back from a customer after she complained it was a forgery. The feds turned their attention to Pierce, suspicious that she had arranged the attack and theft. Outraged, Pierce hired a private investigator, a well-respected Boston police detective, who corroborated that the theft was legitimate and that the injuries Pierce had suffered were real.

Using family connections that Pierce had with then–vice president George Bush, Pierce and the private detective then flew to Washington and met with FBI director William Webster to complain about the handling of the case, and about the FBI agents in Boston. Webster promised to look into the case, but neither the detective nor Pierce ever heard anything more about the matter, and the case remains unsolved to this day.

Eerily, the sketches of the two thieves that a police artist made from Pierce's description look remarkably like the sketches of the two men who, disguised to look like police officers, pulled off the Gardner theft, with one similarly described as taller than the other, and the smaller man more swarthy in appearance than his accomplice.

"I can't tell you it's the same two men," says Pierce now. "But I do believe if the FBI had made more of my case, given it more publicity, maybe people at the museum would have been more careful, more on guard."

There may be a similar problem with the way paintings are transported and sold. In 2006, a man named Charles "Bill" Hofmann was hired by David Rieff, the son of writer and activist Susan Sontag, to transport several storage units in Kingston, New York, filled with artwork and other personal items belonging to Sontag and her former husband following their deaths, to storage space in New York City. Working alone, Hofmann could have helped himself to far more expensive pieces, including signed original photographs taken by Sontag's close friend, Annie Leibovitz, but the painting he took a fancy to, an eighteenth-century portrait of a stuffy-looking British nobleman, happened to catch his fancy. So, rather than placing the piece in the back of the truck with the dozens of other pieces, Hofmann placed it behind his driver's seat and simply brought it home.

In March 2007, Hofmann brought the painting, by old English master Allan Ramsay, to Sotheby's in New York, which, like all reputable auction houses, claims to do a rigorous job of making sure the purported owners of the 10,000 such pieces it sells annually actually do own the pieces.

Even when pressed on the Hofmann case, a Sotheby's spokesperson and its lawyers contend that because of the rigorous protocol it maintained, the auction house still has never sold a stolen painting. In addition to mandating paperwork that proves an individual owns the painting he or she is seeking to auction, the one step that Sotheby's—as well as every other gallery and major auction house—takes before putting any piece up for bid is to check with the Art Loss Register. With offices in both London and New York, the Register maintains a database with the identities of more than 100,000 paintings and other works of art that owners have listed as stolen. Sotheby's maintains that the auction house checked with the Art Loss Register to determine if the Ramsay was listed as stolen. Of course, since Rieff was unaware that the painting was missing, it was not listed in the database of stolen pieces.

Remarkably, Hofmann's lack of documentation didn't stop Sotheby's from accepting it for auction. As a work by an English master, it was decided that the best place for the painting, *Portrait of Lock Rollinson of Chadlington,* would be offered for sale by Sotheby's London office. Sotheby's catalog for sales that day, June 4, 2007, provided an asking price of $30,000–40,000 and described the piece as being in fine condition for a work that had been painted circa 1770.

> The canvas has been lined. The painting is stable and is in need of no further attention. Examination under ultraviolet light reveals a thick varnish which obscures a clear reading. There is evidence of some repaint along the lower right hand portion of the painted oval. There is evidence of some retouching in the sitter's face. It is not possible to penetrate the varnish layer with ultraviolet light, but there would appear to be evidence of older retouching in the background and in the sitter's face.

Hofmann attended the auction—it was his first trip overseas—with his mother, and he was excited as the first bids on the painting came in. But just as quickly, a final bid of $47,000 was soon accepted and it was all over. After Sotheby's took its customary cut, Hofmann was mailed a check for about $34,000.

Hofmann used the money to make repairs to his home, also adding a back deck.

I approached Hofmann not long after the auction, after learning how easy it had been for him to steal the painting and fence it through Sotheby's. He maintained that Sotheby's never pressed him for paperwork after he had told them that the painting was a family heirloom and he had no documentation to prove it. Also, he said that he had gotten possession of the painting legitimately; Rieff had told him for doing such a good job in transporting the artwork and antiques to New York City he could take any piece he wanted.

But Rieff denied that claim, and in March 2011 a federal grand jury indicted Hofmann on two counts of transporting and selling a stolen item. He pleaded guilty to the charges the following year. Hofmann was placed on probation for three years and ordered to make restitution of $34,200 to Sotheby's for bilking them into selling the piece he had stolen.

THE NIGHT BEFORE the FBI's press conference, I couldn't sleep. I tossed and turned, trying to figure out what was going to be said, and wondering if a recovery was about to be announced. What startling development were the FBI and the museum going to share that I had missed in my reporting on the case for the *Boston Globe* for more than a decade?

The basic elements of what had happened the night of the theft—who might have been involved and, more important, where the paintings might be—were always kept confidential. Making such details public could jeopardize the investigation; that was the FBI's familiar refrain. But in March 2013 there was a sense that the FBI might be ready to provide something more, or perhaps even something definite, about what it had discovered.

Richard S. DesLauriers, the special agent in charge of the FBI's Boston office, did not disappoint in his announcement. In a gray pinstripe suit, with a bright yellow tie and his rectangle, wire-rimmed glasses pressed firmly to his temple, and flanked by US attorney Carmen Ortiz and the three investigators who had worked the longest on the case, DesLauriers declared that the FBI knew who had committed the robbery, knew the trail taken to hide at least some of the masterpieces, and even that an attempt had been made in 2002 to sell the pieces in Philadelphia.

My contact had been right. DesLauriers' seven-minute statement on Monday morning, March 18, 2013, at FBI headquarters in Boston was a bombshell. For the first time in the twenty-three-year history of the investigation, the FBI was providing the details of what the hard work of its investigators had yielded and, perhaps even more important, what still needed to be done.

"Some have described the theft as one of the most significant art heists in the nation's history," the square-jawed DesLauriers intoned. "We agree. Today the investigation has had many twists and turns, promising leads and dead ends. But over the years, the FBI has never relented. Instead we persevere, analyzing and reviewing thousands of leads, interviewing many, methodically allowing us to move people in or out as suspects.

"Remaining tenacious and not giving up is the key to solving these cases," he went on. "Today, on the twenty-third anniversary of the theft, we are pleased to announce the FBI has made significant investigative progress in the search of the stolen art from the Isabella Stewart Gardner Museum. For the first time we can say with a high degree of confidence we've determined, in the years since the theft, the art was transported to Connecticut and to the Philadelphia area."

It was a classic public relations announcement that stressed the positive elements of what the FBI had learned—while leaning a little on the truth. "We know finding stolen art often spans decades, or longer. A Cezanne stolen from Stockbridge, Massachusetts, in 1978 was recovered twenty-one years later. And five years after that, this office recovered the five works that were stolen with that piece. Remaining tenacious and not giving up is the key to solving these cases," DesLauriers declared.

The truth is that the recovery of the Cezanne in 1999 was engineered by Julian Radcliffe, a British investigator whose Art Loss Register tracked stolen art for the insurance industry, and who never worked for the FBI. It was Radcliffe whose unwavering efforts had located the individual responsible for stashing the stolen paintings, and it was Radcliffe who had followed that trail like a bloodhound to the ultimate recovery, without which the FBI likely would not have located the companion works. In fact, when they were offered a chance to get the Cezanne back in exchange for letting the other works go, the FBI seemed prepared to take it. It was Radcliffe who insisted that all six works be returned.

In total, DesLauriers' remarks about the Gardner theft had the assembled reporters scrambling, asking for details: Who had committed the robbery and stashed the paintings all these years? What had happened in Philadelphia in 2002 to make the FBI certain a sale had been attempted? And if nothing had been heard of the paintings' whereabouts for more than a decade, why was the FBI so certain of its information?

But DesLauriers resisted, saying giving out further details could jeopardize the FBI's ongoing efforts to recover the paintings.

Despite the troubling lack of details to the handful of reporters who had followed the Gardner case closely over the years, DesLauriers' press conference was featured by all the major television news outlets and received front-page coverage in newspapers across the nation. So intense was the coverage that it soon became clear that there was another reason for DesLauriers' announcement, something other than giving the public an update on the status of the investigation. The FBI needed the public's help.

Clearly the FBI had entered into the "final chapter" of the investigation, but the goal here was not to arrest the criminals responsible but, rather, to recover the stolen pieces. For that it desperately needed the public's help.

"It is likely over the years that someone, a friend, loved one, or relative, has seen the art hanging on the wall, placed above a mantle, or stored in an attic," DesLauriers had said. "We want that person to call us.

"The FBI is not content to know just the general location of the art years ago, or the identity of those who committed the theft," DesLauriers said in wrapping up his statement. "To close the book on this theft, we need to recover the art and return them to its rightful owner. We call upon the American public to assist us in this investigation as they have so many times before."

Although DesLauriers chose not to be specific, the most recent instance of the FBI asking for the public's help had resulted in the arrest of notorious Boston mobster James "Whitey" Bulger. The FBI had asked that anyone who recognized Bulger's girlfriend, who had been at his side for more than fifteen years, call a toll-free hotline. A woman who had been their neighbor in the Santa Monica, California, apartment complex where the pair had been living under assumed names alerted the FBI, and within days a capture was made.

It made sense, therefore, that such a public appeal would be tried in the Gardner case. But the FBI needed to maximize the campaign, and the press conference was the answer. Thirteen pieces of artwork were stolen from the Isabella Stewart Gardner Museum on March 18, 1990, and many weren't well known to the public at large. For twenty-three years there had been no "proof of life" of a single piece, and while people might recall what the two most valuable pieces—Rembrandt's *Storm on the Sea of Galilee* and Vermeer's *The Concert*—looked like, the lesser works were largely unknown. Any one of them could provide a trail that could lead to the recovery of the major pieces, if not all of them, so the FBI needed to make certain that as many people as possible looked at the website dedicated to the case or at least the advertisements that featured them.

Providing a further sense that the aim of the press conference was a public appeal was US Attorney Ortiz, who followed DesLauriers to the microphone. Ortiz stressed that there were two incentives for those to come forward with information: They would not be prosecuted for any involvement they might have had in the theft or concealment of the paintings, and if their information led to a recovery, they could make a valid claim on the $5 million reward the Gardner Museum offered for returning the artwork.

Having reported on the theft since the late 1990s, I, like DesLauriers, yearned for a final chapter to be written, for the paintings to be returned to their rightful places at the museum. But I feared that without a trial, it was up to independent reporting to tell the story of how and why they had been stolen and where they had been kept all these years. Otherwise, it would mean that Boston's last best secret would go untold, and that all of us—and history—would be denied the chance of learning the lessons this extraordinary event had taught us.

Although DesLauriers and Ortiz mentioned no names, sources familiar with the investigation put names and faces to those said to be involved: David A. Turner, Robert A. Guarente, and Robert Gentile.

I knew these individuals by name, but why did the FBI now believe that all roads in the Gardner case led to them? What was their connection to the robbery? As I would soon learn, it all started with a failed lie detector test and three hundred tablets of prescription pain reliever.

CHAPTER SIX

THE SECRET
IN THE SHED

R OBERT V. GENTILE was losing control of the situation, and he
knew it. For months the aging hood from the Connecticut
suburbs around Hartford had been promising to aid the FBI in
its investigation into the whereabouts of the nearly half billion
dollars' worth of paintings stolen in the 1990 Gardner Museum
heist. But those promises had led nowhere.

Instead, during the time he had been helping them, the
same federal agents were arranging to bust him for selling
more than three hundred tablets of Oxycontin, Dilaudid, and
Percocet—all pain relievers he had been prescribed by doctors
for his back pain—to an undercover informant. That way, if
he backed out of cooperating with them on the Gardner score,
they could arrest him and pressure him to talk anyway.

The room in the US Attorney's Office on the third floor of
450 Main Street in downtown Hartford was chaotic, crammed

with prosecutors, FBI agents, and investigators that day in April 2012. They knew they had Gentile in a tight spot. Gentile had just been indicted on drug charges and, even though there may have been extenuating circumstances, he was well into his seventies and still faced the real prospect of a long prison sentence, one that in his health he might never return from.

To Gentile and his lawyer, A. Ryan McGuigan, it seemed the only way around those charges was to submit to a lie detector test. If Gentile could pass the test, he thought, it might just convince the federal agents and prosecutors bearing down on him that what he had been telling them—that he didn't know anything about the whereabouts of the Gardner artwork—was true and they would drop the drug charges against him, or at least let him off easy.

The whole thing had started two years before, in 2010, when the widow of Gentile's old friend Robert Guarente told investigators that before her husband died in 2004 he had given two, maybe three paintings to Gentile for safekeeping. They may have been from the theft at the Gardner Museum.

"Sure, I knew Bobby Guarente," Gentile had told the investigators when they originally approached him. "And yeah, maybe we did talk about the Gardner case. But it was only to talk about how great it would be to get that $5 million reward. Guarente never had any of those paintings, and he certainly never gave me any of them."

As Gentile walked into the interrogation room at the Hartford federal building and surveyed the determined faces, he thought to himself, *The only way of getting them to drop these charges against me is to convince them I'm telling the truth.*

"Go ahead," he told them. "Hook me up." And they did.

Ronald Barndollar, the retired FBI agent who was called in to conduct the polygraph exam, began things on a serious note, advising Gentile of his need to tell the truth. Then he asked the first question:

"Did you know beforehand that the Gardner Museum was going to be robbed?" asked Barndollar.

"No," Gentile answered.

In an adjacent room the polygraph machine registered that Gentile's answer was a lie.

Gentile was shown pictures of the thirteen works of art that had been stolen. With each one he was asked: "Did you ever have possession of any of the stolen artwork?"

"No," Gentile answered again, and again the polygraph machine registered each time that Gentile was lying.

"Do you know the location of any of those paintings?"

"No," Gentile answered. And again, the polygraph machine registered the likelihood that Gentile was lying.

When the exam was over, Barndollar excused himself and came back in a few minutes with the results: Gentile had been lying in response to every question.

The investigators let out a howl in unison. "This guy is gonna rot in jail if he doesn't give us something," Gentile recalls one saying.

McGuigan looked over at assistant US attorney Peter Markle, the veteran federal prosecutor who was assisting in handling the Gentile case, and asked if he could have a little time with his client. When they were alone, he shot Gentile a stern look that said, "What the hell are you doing?" McGuigan's hope that the polygraph test might do Gentile some good had disappeared fast.

Gentile was in failing health. He didn't want to die behind bars. He knew his only hope was in the lie-detector results convincing the authorities that his claims of innocence regarding the Gardner heist weren't just the rantings of a desperate man. This was it. It was, so to speak, his moment of truth.

Gentile reached over and grabbed McGuigan's arm. "I'm telling the truth; it's that goddamned machine," Gentile told him. "They've rigged it to make me look like a liar. Tell them I want to take it again. I've got an idea. You'll see."

Gentile's idea: In taking the test again, he would concoct a story that he had seen one of the stolen paintings in the past.

Within minutes, the whole procedure was repeated. The images of the stolen pieces were again shown on a screen in front of him. As each one scanned past, Gentile was asked if he had ever seen the piece after it had been stolen.

Vermeer's *The Concert*?

No.

Rembrandt's *Storm on the Sea of Galilee*?

No.

Rembrandt's *Lady and Gentleman in Black*?

No.

The miniature self-portrait by Rembrandt? There was a long pause. The room suddenly went still.

"Yes," said Gentile. And on this question, the polygraph registered he was telling the truth.

"What are you talking about?" one of the investigators asked Gentile, with an almost manic sound in his voice. "When did you see this? Where did you see it?"

Like criminals of all stripes and at all levels, Gentile prided himself on never snitching, especially not in front of a room full of feds. But Elene Guarente had dragged him into this by implicating him in hiding three of the stolen paintings, so he figured the least he could do was return the favor.

"Elene Guarente showed it to me," Gentile said, referring to the widow of Robert Guarente, the mob soldier whose reach extended from Boston to Maine. "It was a long time ago. It was tiny. Like a postage stamp. She pulled it out of her bra, where she was hiding it, to show me. She told me it was going to provide for her retirement. Maybe get her a house in Florida with it."

The FBI agents and federal prosecutors were stunned. They looked around the room at each other, in disbelief at what they'd just heard. Barndollar, the FBI agent running the polygraph examination, excused himself and retrieved the results from the other room: it showed that Gentile had answered honestly when he told them he had seen the miniature Rembrandt self-portrait before. As far as the machine was concerned, Gentile was telling the truth.

The name Elene Guarente wasn't new to federal agents. In fact, just two years before, she'd told them that her husband had handed Gentile several paintings in the parking lot of a Portland, Maine, restaurant. The feds had dug into Gentile's background and discovered he had deep ties to organized crime figures in Connecticut and may have been operating a loan-shark business there. After that they'd tracked Gentile's activities closely, waiting for the right moment when they could put the pressure on him to find out more about his mob dealings.

But now, in the face of Gentile's stunning admission, federal agents who had labored on the Gardner investigation for more than two decades had in their midst a suspect who was at the very least involved in hiding the artwork.

Following the test, McGuigan remained convinced that Gentile's disastrous showing had more to do with the raucous setting in which the exam was given than with Gentile's veracity. But he realized he needed more than ever to convince the federal agents of that, so he asked for one final meeting in the US attorney's office to try to convince the federal investigators that Gentile was being honest. Just Durham and James Lawton, the FBI agent who had labored for two years on the Gentile case, would attend this one. Gentile would be brought in from the state prison where he had been held since his February arrest, along with his wife, Patricia, son Bobby, and daughter Donna.

To try to make the atmosphere more amenable for his client, McGuigan ordered special sandwiches from Gentile's favorite Italian restaurant. The feds brought their own sandwiches—from a local Subway.

From the outset, McGuigan did most of the talking, stressing to Gentile that this was his last chance to assist the investigators in their search for the missing Gardner paintings.

"They are convinced you're not telling them everything, and I'm telling you that this may be your only way out," Gentile remembers McGuigan saying. "These people are serious. With these charges you're facing and the condition of your health, if they get a conviction, they can put you away for the rest of your life."

If he knew what happened to the paintings, this was the time to come clean. "This is more important than just paintings, Bob. This is about history. This is about humanity. There have been millions of Bobby Gentiles and Ryan McGuigans on this earth and there will be millions after us . . . but there's only one Rembrandt."

Gentile, with his head down, responded: "I know, I know, I know, it's important, I know."

Gentile then picked his head up and looked sadly over at his wife and grown children, and McGuigan picked up on it.

"You'll never get to hug your wife again, or your kids or grandkids," he said. "Give these people what they want. Tell them what you know about the paintings."

Gentile put his head back down. Then put his hands, big and rough from a lifetime of working in the paving industry, over his face. The room fell silent for a few seconds as he sobbed.

"In your right mind, do you think I would hold out if I knew something?" Gentile asked. "I know there's a five million–dollar reward here. Do you think I would deny my family five million dollars and get these charges off my back if I could? I'll tell you again, I don't know anything, and whoever is telling you different is lying."

The meeting broke up soon after, but not before Lawton, who had begun the investigation, got in the final word:

"What your lawyer told you is right: If you're convicted of these charges, you're going to die in prison."

Gentile went back to prison and waited to head back to court to face the drug charges.

A few days later, just after the morning rush hour, a squad of FBI agents descended on his house in Manchester, a few miles east of downtown Hartford. More than two dozen agents surveyed his front and back yards, looking for signs of recently dug holes or anything else that might point to hidden treasures. They did likewise inside the house, going through every room, every drawer, and every nook and cranny—the basement included—looking for any clues that would prove Gentile had any association with the stolen paintings.

The search gave the investigators proof that they were on the right track. Down in the cluttered basement, among a pile of old newspapers, the investigators found a *Boston Herald* newspaper that reported on the extraordinary theft. A sheet of typewriter paper was tucked into the newspaper. On the sheet was written the names of the thirteen pieces that had been stolen from the Gardner Museum. Alongside the names was scratched the amount that each might draw on the black market.

The find surprised even McGuigan. Even though he was never convinced Gentile had anything to do with the stolen masterpieces, McGuigan thought to himself, maybe it had been a good idea that he had signed a separate contract with Gentile. It stated that he would represent Gentile as he cooperated with the authorities, and if it led to a recovery, McGuigan's office would receive 40 percent of the $5 million reward offered by the Gardner.

McGuigan was returning from court on another case when he got word about the FBI raid on Gentile's house. He headed straight to his client's house, slowing only to take a call from a newspaper reporter asking for comment on the search.

"All I know right now is that they've got enough agents in my client's backyard to fight a war," McGuigan told the reporter. "They've got everything with them. Shovels, rakes, backhoes," and then jokingly added: "Three dogs, two cats, and a ferret."

Such was the excitement surrounding the story that within seconds the newspaper had included in its online account of the raid that a ferret was being used in the search. For the first time in more than ten years a sense of anticipation built that the masterpieces would be recovered, in a Connecticut backyard less than one hundred yards from a busy highway, no less.

When McGuigan arrived at the Gentile home he quickly sought out Brian Kelly, the assistant US attorney from Boston who was overseeing the Gardner investigation. Inside the house, McGuigan saw Gentile's wife, sitting quietly on the living room sofa as agents walked briskly throughout the house.

One agent handed McGuigan the warrant that had been signed that morning by a federal judicial officer to authorize the search of the house and backyard. Realizing that a backyard shed had not been included specifically in the search, the agents had gotten a second warrant that authorized that search.

McGuigan, who had been a prosecutor before joining his father's law firm in a high-rise in downtown Hartford, immediately made his way to a swarm of reporters and cameramen already huddled there on Frances Street, behind the yellow police tape, eager to report that a major break in the Gardner heist was imminent.

Like any good lawyer with a high-profile client, McGuigan looked for the scrum of microphones to try to get his position stated. Appearing calm but stern, McGuigan spoke to the cameras: "This case comes down to the fact that this guy sold his own painkillers to some kid who was working for the FBI, so

The FBI was convinced that one or more masterpieces were hidden in a ditch dug under a false floor in this shed in scenic Manchester, Connecticut—in the backyard of Robert Gentile. But a thorough search in May 2012 turned up nothing.

they could search his house," he said. "My client knows nothing about the whereabouts of any paintings."

Gentile's son shared McGuigan's confidence that his father knew nothing about the paintings' whereabouts. He assured the agents that while his father was a pack rat, he did not have the connections or the wherewithal to hide such priceless art. The only place he could imagine his father hiding anything valuable was in his shed in the backyard.

Whereabouts in the shed, one agent asked him casually. And Robert Jr., who shared his father's softer side, gave him a straight answer—his father had placed a false floor in the front of the shed, and beneath it, he had dug a deep pit, and inside the pit there would be a large plastic, Tupperware-type container.

Whatever's important will be in a plastic container inside that pit, the younger Gentile told the agents.

His instructions set the agents off into a mad scramble, in which they tore up the false floor inside the shed, and found the deep pit under it and the big plastic container inside—a big empty plastic container.

Shown the container, young Gentile had one more piece of compelling information: A few years before, there had been a severe rainstorm in the area; water had flooded their backyard and gotten into the shed and even into the ditch beneath the shed's false floor. Whatever had been in the ditch had been destroyed, Gentile's son told the agents, adding that he had never seen his father as upset in his life as he was about the loss. When I asked Gentile about it, he said he didn't recall the incident but thought it could have involved a couple of small motors getting wet.

A few days later, federal agents and Anthony Amore, the Gardner Museum's security director, brought Gentile back to the Hartford federal building where he had taken the lie-detector test a month before.

One of the FBI agents got right up in Gentile's face. "We know what happened," he said. "Your son told us about the shed and how the pit got flooded."

"Tell us where those canvases are," Amore pleaded, as-suming the role of "good cop" in the situation. "Even if the paintings are damaged or destroyed, I'll see to it that you get a share of the reward money. Just show us the canvases."

Gentile had been thrust into the middle of what federal investigators believed was their biggest break in their long, arduous pursuit of the masterpieces stolen in the early hours of March 18, 1990. Perhaps too ashamed to acknowledge that the paintings had been ruined while in his possession, or more likely worried about the consequences that might stem from such an admission, Gentile held firm.

"I don't know anything," he said.

"THAT DAY RUINED MY LIFE FOREVER," Gentile tells me, sitting in the living room of the modest ranch-style home in suburban Hartford that he's lived in for years with his wife and two children. He has been home from federal prison for a week, and our conversation is the first time he has ever spoken publicly.

I'd written to Gentile while he was serving a thirty-month sentence in federal prison in Otisville, New York, and had asked him if I could come visit him in prison to talk about his case and the authorities' interest in his ties to the Gardner heist. I had caught his eye by giving him a thumbs-up during a break in one of his court hearings. "Who's the older reporter, with the gray hair?" he asked McGuigan.

He wrote back. "Wait until I get home in January, and call my house."

In fact it could have been a lot worse for Gentile. Assistant US attorney John Durham had asked that Gentile be sentenced to a total of forty-six to fifty-seven months in prison, a term recommended by the sentencing guidelines. But US district judge Robert N. Chatigny appeared to heed McGuigan's insistence in court that investigators had focused on Gentile to squeeze him on the Gardner investigation. As a result Chatigny said that Gentile's poor health and that of his wife deserved to be considered. He set Gentile's prison term at a total of thirty months.

Emerging from the courtroom, McGuigan said, "Mr. Gentile is pleased with the sentence. He thinks it is fair."

Durham refused comment.

In late January, I drove to Gentile's Connecticut home and introduced myself. Although he still walked with the help of a cane, he looked more rested and clear-eyed than when I'd seen him in court. He said he needed the cane because he was still in pain from a long-ago back injury. He wore a bracelet on his ankle to ensure he complied with the terms of his probation, that he remain inside his house for three months after his release from prison.

We talked for a long time. Gentile answered all of my questions, casting doubt on the FBI's belief that he was the last person to know the whereabouts of the Gardner masterpieces. Then, near the end of the interview, Gentile told me to shut off my tape recorder.

"Talk to me man-to-man." I shut off the recorder.

"I'm a man of my word," he said, looking without expression at me. "If I tell you something, you can believe me." He then proceeded to ask me what he might gain from the cooperation he was giving me.

I told him that if he was looking for money, I didn't have any to give. But if I wrote his account straight enough, and was able to corroborate that the feds had set him up in the drug case to get him to change his story about what he knew about the Gardner paintings, it might attract documentary filmmakers who would pay him to tell his story.

I sensed that Gentile was trying to tell me something about himself and the paintings, perhaps even to withdraw his denial that he had nothing to do with them. "If you've got another story to tell, then I would be willing to ask my publisher to rewrite our contract so you would get a share of the proceeds," I told him. "It would be an extraordinary story and I am sure it would be a best seller if it led to the recovery of any of the paintings, but you would have to acknowledge that all these denials have been lies, and what was behind them."

Gentile put his head down for thirty seconds. *I might be on the verge of something historic here,* I thought to myself. He waited and then looked at me with a gaze as strong and steeled-eyed as I'd seen so far.

"That's just it," Gentile said, motioning that I could turn my recorder back on. "They set me up, and they ruined my life. My daughter died while I was in jail. Prison officials wouldn't even let me visit her before she died. And when I got out I found out the $950 a month I'd been receiving in Social Security benefits had been cut off because I'd been convicted of a federal crime.

"What I told you stands. They set me up and ruined my life." The moment had passed.

As if to prove his point, Gentile gave me the key to his shed. Yes, he admitted, he kept valuables in containers in the ditch beneath the false floor. But only pieces of equipment or small motors that he had bought. Nothing illegal or stolen, and certainly not the Gardner paintings. I bundled up and crunched through the snow in his backyard and opened the shed's doors. A new wooden floor had replaced the one the feds dug up, but the large plastic bins his son Bobby had described to the investigators were still inside. Some were filled with hoses, others with yard equipment. None seemed large enough to have held the tubes that could have contained large paintings.

ALTHOUGH ROBERT GENTILE was never identified by name, it was clear he was at the center of the bombshell announcement that Richard S. DesLauriers made in March 2013, on the twenty-third anniversary of the Gardner Museum theft.

"With a high degree of confidence we believe those responsible for the theft were members of a criminal organization with a base in the mid-Atlantic states and New England," he told the assembled press.

DesLauriers stressed that while his agents had had no good leads about the artwork in more than a decade, their investigation had made them certain the works had been brought to Connecticut and then Philadelphia. DesLauriers' remarks made front-page news around the world. For the first time since the 1990 theft the FBI had given details, scant though they were, about what their years of investigation had uncovered. After more than twenty years of chasing false leads, whether provided by outright liars or others chasing the reward of the century, the FBI finally had information they felt strong enough to announce to the world. That they had determined who the robbers were and had tracked the stolen artwork to Connecticut and Philadelphia was remarkable. That they weren't releasing more details of the identities of those involved, they said firmly, had more to do with the sensitivity of the investigation than its certainty.

While no one had been named as suspects at DesLauriers' press conference, newspapers including the *Boston Globe* and *Hartford Courant* were soon quoting sources familiar with the investigation, putting names to those said to be involved: David A. Turner, orchestrating the theft; Robert A. Guarente, in charge of hiding the stolen masterpieces; and then Gentile as the fence.

Ample information allowed enterprising reporters to connect the dots DesLauriers laid out. Turner, with his ties to the Rossetti gang and Louis Royce, knew of the museum's vulnerability to theft. Having lost his father as a teenager, Turner had appreciated that Guarente had treated him like a son and had great respect for the aging mobster's deep ties to organized crime. Guarente and Gentile were close, and Gentile readily acknowledged that he'd cooked for a weekend card game that Guarente organized at a house in suburban Boston and that Guarente had used the place as a base for his cocaine trafficking operation in the late 1990s.

As for the FBI, DesLauriers hoped the announcement would have two immediate reactions that might lead to a breakthrough recovery. First, that the public would take his advice and look in their attics and garages to see if anything had been hidden there. And second, that someone in the underworld, who might have had secret information on the paintings, would make a call that would be picked up on one of the FBI's many standing wiretaps.

The announcement created tremendous media attention and brought numerous calls to Boston's FBI office. But within a month all had been followed up to no avail, and the sense of an inevitable recovery soon faded. By that time the public's attention, not to mention that of DesLauriers and every other FBI agent assigned to the Boston office, had rightfully shifted to another case: the Boston Marathon bombing. The FBI's press person began referring to the Gardner announcement as a "publicity event," and both DesLauriers and the head of the FBI's criminal division declined to answer questions on how credible the information in their "significant investigative process" had actually been.

In fact, the lines connecting the dots set out by DesLauriers were blurry and full of gaps. And the most important unexplained link was Philadelphia. Only a circumstantial case could be built that would tie Gentile to Philadelphia, though, I found, it did involve his ties to Guarente.

The cocaine that Guarente was indicted for trafficking in 1999 had allegedly come from the Merlino crime family in Philadelphia, and both Guarente and Robert Luisi Jr., his partner in the cocaine ring, were alleged to be made members of the Merlino crime family. Luisi himself was entrenched in Boston's mob scene.

In a grisly public scene that ranks among the nastiest in Boston's history, Luisi's father, half-brother, and cousin were gunned down by another reputed mob member in 1995 while having lunch at a popular Boston lunch spot. Several years later, Luisi and Guarente were indicted for being part of a twelve-member ring that was selling cocaine throughout Boston.

"I drove Luisi to Philadelphia," Gentile admitted to me that day at his house. But it had nothing to do with any cocaine dealings, he said. He said he was unaware that Guarente and Luisi were running a major cocaine operation out of a house in suburban Boston—he only visited them on weekends to cook for them and run a round-the-clock high-roller card game out of the house.

Gentile said he had driven Luisi to Philadelphia on several occasions as Luisi was looking to expand his loan-sharking operations—but not cocaine—to Philadelphia and he needed permission of Merlino and his top guys. Could the topic of the Gardner paintings come up while in the car with Luisi or meeting with the Merlino gang in Philadelphia? I asked Gentile. "I didn't speak to Luisi—or anyone else in Philadelphia—about the Gardner paintings during our drives," Gentile said. "Why would I talk to them about that?"

But there is little doubt that Luisi was talking to the federal authorities about his conversations with Gentile. When called before a federal grand jury, Luisi testified that Gentile had spoken to him about the possibility of putting a crew together to knock over armored car deliveries to and from the Foxwoods casino in Connecticut. Did he also talk about the Gardner case and Gentile? Luisi isn't saying. After initially agreeing to continue to cooperate with federal investigators in their probe of the Boston underworld, Luisi pulled back, testifying that he had "found Jesus" and wanted to serve out his time in prison counseling others.

Luisi was later released when his conviction was overturned on appeal, but whether he had spoken about the Gardner paintings with Gentile and mob leaders in Philadelphia could not be determined, as he did not return phone calls. As of this writing, he is said to be working on a book about his religious experiences.

And while Gentile is adamant that he never had possession of any of the Gardner paintings, it is easy to understand what leads investigators to believe he is lying. The FBI had found the list of the stolen paintings, handwritten on a sheet of typewriter paper inside the *Boston Herald* for March 19, 1990, reporting on the Gardner heist. In all, the amounts listed that the paintings could fetch on the black market added up to almost $8 million.

It was such a compelling piece of evidence tying Gentile to possible possession of the artwork that it was cited by assistant US attorney John Durham at one of Gentile's federal court hearings in Hartford. I wanted to know why Gentile would draw up such a list if he wasn't planning on selling the paintings on the black market.

Sitting in his living room, in his modest suburban Hartford home, Gentile told me a story too convoluted and complicated to be false, and the account was corroborated by an associate, who had been involved in the theft of a Rembrandt from a Worcester art museum in the 1970s, who went on to tell me the list had been drawn up by him, not Gentile.

CHAPTER SEVEN

AT THE CENTER OF THE FBI'S WEB

DURING THE MOB'S HEYDAY in Boston, between 1970 and 1985, just about every criminal in the city believed that the return of a valuable stolen artwork could shorten a prison sentence or even make it go away. Even though the authorities delivered far less, that's what mobsters believed. And one of those hoods, Florian "Al" Monday, knew his way around stolen masterpieces better than most. In 1972, he engineered the heist of a Rembrandt and three other pieces from the Worcester Art Museum, but after a guard was shot during what was a seemingly foolproof plan, and a panic ensued among his co-conspirators, Monday was convinced to turn the artwork in.

For those in a legal bind, especially those who face prosecution for white-collar crimes, the return of a piece of stolen art offers the hope that prosecutors will be willing to give them a break at trial or in sentencing, or even consideration if they're already behind bars. The Gardner case was no different.

After the Gardner Museum theft, Monday, with his host of underworld contacts, reached out to anyone who would listen with a simple proposition: If enough money could be raised, he knew people who knew people who could facilitate the return of the paintings. He was so convincing, in fact, that then–US senator John F. Kerry wrote a letter urging others to assist him, and the US attorney for Massachusetts wrote to Monday assuring him of immunity from prosecution if his dealings put him in contact with any criminals.

This Hollywood-style deal-making is the sort that has lain just beneath the surface of the Gardner case from almost the beginning, and it's also what makes the investigators' work so frustrating. Too many of these insiders are lying, and every thief promises more than he can deliver, whether it's money or concrete evidence of the existence or even whereabouts of the Gardner paintings.

It's also just the sort of situation to attract people like Monday and Paul Papasadero, a sign painter and amateur artist from the working-class town of Milford, not far outside of Boston. In 2001, they approached Robert Gentile with a proposition: Two lawyers from western Massachusetts were being investigated for fraud and they had intimated that they were willing to pay dearly to broker the return of the Gardner paintings, believing it would win them special consideration from the prosecutors in their case.

"Whatever it takes, Paulie says these guys are willing to pay it," Monday said.

This wasn't the first time Monday had tried to broker the return of the Gardner art. Several years before, in 1997, he'd heard through the grapevine that Bobby Guarente, the convicted bank robber and Boston underworld figure, had a connection to the stolen pieces. He tried to reach Guarente but nothing ever came of his attempts. Now he was willing to try again.

Papasadero knew Gentile could reach Guarente, so he—or Monday, depending on whom you believe—approached Gentile and asked for Bobby Guarente's phone number.

"If Guarente can come up with a photograph of one or more of the stolen paintings, I'll pay him $50,000, no questions asked," Papasadero told Gentile.

"These are valuable paintings," Monday, a withered, white-haired man who looks more like a shuffleboard champ than an art thief, said he told Gentile when they met. He explained some of the history of the pieces—to deaf ears, he thought—and he wrote out on a blank piece of paper what people might be willing to pay on the black market for the individual items. At the top he wrote the names of the most valuable two: Vermeer's *The Concert*, $4 million, and Rembrandt's *Storm on the Sea of Galilee*, $2 million.

Gentile was excited. This was easy, he thought. He called Guarente and told him about Monday's offer.

"Sounds good," Guarente told him. "I'll contact this guy when I've got the photographs."

Thinking Guarente would be directly contacting Monday and Papasadero, Gentile was surprised to get a letter from Guarente just a little while later with photographs inside. He called Papasadero, who raced over to Gentile's house that night. Instead of $50,000, however, he brought only $10,000. Regardless, he hardly got his money's worth.

When Papasadero opened the envelope, he found that Guarente hadn't taken photographs of the original paintings. Instead, he had gone to a library and found an encyclopedia reference to the Gardner theft and took photographs of the images showing the stolen paintings.

"I don't know why Bobby [Guarente] wanted to get me involved in something like that, but the guy, Papasadero, just threw the photographs back at me and walked out," Gentile said. "I can't blame the guy. He didn't get anything like what he was looking for."

The list Monday drew up showing what each of the thirteen pieces of Gardner artwork might bring on the black market would come back to haunt Gentile. It was that list, which he kept folded into a *Boston Herald* newspaper from the day after the theft, that was found during the raid of Gentile's home in May 2012 among the junk in his basement. Without any mention of its origins, leaving reporters at least to believe it had been drawn up by Gentile, the federal prosecutor used the list to seek a long prison sentence against Gentile and raise suspicions of his connection to the Gardner heist.

————————

FOR AT LEAST THREE YEARS before the FBI's March 2013 announcement, Richard DesLauriers, the agent in charge of the investigation into the Gardner heist, had been looking into the ties between Gentile, Bobby Guarente, and David Turner, a middleclass Boston kid who'd found his calling in life as a mob soldier, as the key to solving the case.

As outlined by federal investigators and sources, the triumvirate was responsible for organizing the theft and then stashing the artwork all these years. This had all come together for the FBI after Guarente's sixty-three-year-old former wife, desperate for money, saw one of the billboards the FBI had put up on the roads leading north out of Boston asking for tips on the Gardner robbery. "Help us recover the stolen pieces and we'll pay you $5 million," the billboards announced, tantalizingly.

Forget those millions, Elene Guarente thought when she saw them. She just needed $1,000 to fix the radiator in her car. One way or another, she figured the best way of getting her hands on the money she needed was to talk about what her late ex-husband had once shown her.

In the early 1990s, as they settled into their new homestead in Madison, Maine, Bobby Guarente had shown Elene a painting of a woman sitting in a rocking chair with her head turned to the side. Although she later said she told investigators and a grand jury that they didn't look like either of the two paintings stolen from the Gardner Museum in which women were seated in chairs, Rembrandt's *Lady and Gentleman in Black* and Vermeer's *The Concert*, she remembered how proud Guarente was of the painting.

"Isn't it the most beautiful thing you've ever seen?" he'd asked her, taking it out of a heavy-duty rolling tube. "Do you have any idea of how much it's worth?"

"I wouldn't give you ten dollars for it," she'd fired back. "It's all so gloomy. I don't want it hanging up here in our house."

Guarente used the Maine home as his weekend residence and during the week stayed with a friend outside of Boston. He was a frequent visitor to an auto repair garage that his longtime friend Carmello Merlino operated in Dorchester, and out of which Merlino ran a number of criminal enterprises, including dealing cocaine.

In late 1997, Merlino began talking at his garage about the possibility of being able to recover the Gardner paintings and, according to an undercover informant, made it known that Bobby Guarente was among several individuals who could make the recovery happen. Guarente and Merlino had served time together in Massachusetts prisons with legendary art thief Myles Connor while he was completing a twenty-year sentence after he'd pleaded guilty to involvement in multiple Boston-area bank robberies in 1969.

But Guarente's move to Maine did not cut him off from his criminal associates. According to Maine state police reports from the early 1990s, Guarente was being investigated for drug trafficking in Massachusetts and Maine, and criminal associates from Boston, such as David Turner and Stephen Rossetti, were frequent visitors to his Maine home for weekend hunting excursions.

An FBI report attested to Guarente's involvement with organized crime figures. During the battle for control of Boston's underworld in the 1980s and '90s, he was aligned with Frank "Cadillac Frank" Salemme. Guarente was designated by his bosses to make it clear to Richard "The Pig" DeVincent, whom he knew from prison in the early 1980s, that he needed to stop associating with a rival gang seeking the same power. DeVincent did not heed Guarente's advice and was shot to death in 1996, an execution witnessed by Guarente and a member of the Rossetti crime gang, according to the FBI. Guarente was quoted by an informant as saying that another witness's gun had jammed in shooting DeVincent and that "it was a good thing my gun was working properly."

By this time, Guarente had gotten involved in a major drug trafficking network, bringing cocaine up from Philadelphia and distributing it out of a house he was renting in Waltham, making it possible that through this network word was received in Philadelphia that paintings stolen from the Gardner Museum were for sale in the early 2000s.

The FBI refuses to say how they put this together—whether it came from an informant or was picked up on a wire. But there is no doubt that Guarente was associated with the network, selling for established buyers and looking for new ones, using cocaine supplied via Philadelphia.

A thirty-one-page affidavit described Guarente's involvement: An individual who owed Guarente $70,000 from previous cocaine purchases agreed to go undercover for the Boston office of the Drug Enforcement Administration in an investigation of Guarente.

On numerous occasions, over a six-month period beginning in August 1997, the informant paid thousands of dollars to Guarente for cocaine deliveries. Some of the deals took place in Maine, though most were completed in and around Waltham, Massachusetts.

Guarente told the informant that his partner in the operation was Robert C. Luisi Jr., a made member of the Philadelphia mob, and that he spent some of his time collecting on debts owed to Luisi. Although he was not named in the affidavit, which framed the indictment against Guarente, Robert Gentile, the man the FBI believes last had possession of the stolen Gardner paintings, later acknowledged in interviews with me that he worked for Guarente and Luisi at their Waltham hideout and even drove Luisi to some of his meetings in Philadelphia.

But Gentile denies knowing that cocaine was being trafficked out of the residence. He says his purpose there was solely to run high-stakes card games that Guarente allowed at the house, as well as to cook for the players and associates.

"No one knew how to run a card game, so that's what I did for them," Gentile told me.

If Guarente had access to the stolen Gardner paintings, he certainly had a pressing reason to tell federal authorities about it. Immediately after his arrest for cocaine trafficking in March 1998, Guarente told DEA investigators that he was willing to cooperate with their investigation. On being questioned about Luisi's role, according to the affidavit, "Guarente admitted he was aware that Luisi was involved in the large-scale distribution of cocaine."

Days later, though, Guarente notified the DEA he was no longer interested in cooperating. He was sentenced to five years in prison, and released on probation in August 2002. He returned to Maine and his wife, Elene. At some point in the next year or so, according to Elene's account, Guarente decided to put together a lunch in nearby Portland with his old friend Bobby Gentile and Gentile's wife. It was after that lunch, Elene says, that Guarente handed over the paintings to Gentile.

Elene's story implicating her late ex-husband and Robert Gentile is the most detailed account of what happened to the Gardner paintings. She testified before a federal grand jury in Boston in 2010, giving details consistent with what she originally told Geoff Kelly, the FBI's lead agent on the case, and Anthony Amore, the museum's security chief, at her home in Maine.

But what was apparently never told to the grand jury—or Kelly and Amore—was an account given me by Guarente's best friend in Maine, Earle E. Berghman. Several years before Elene told authorities that her late husband had held onto the Gardner paintings, Berghman tried—without success—to make the same connection.

According to Berghman, about a year after Bobby Guarente's death in 2004, he was approached by Guarente's daughter and told that she recalled her father owning a painting that was similar to Rembrandt's *Storm on the Sea of Galilee*. "In fact, she told me that Bobby had it hanging in the living room of the house he lived in with her," Berghman said. "I'm telling you and you can mark my words, Bobby Guarente is at the center of this web."

Berghman, as it turns out, knew Guarente well. While he says they got to know each other hanging out and hunting in the woods surrounding their homes in central Maine, the state police had their eyes on them and other associates. According to Maine state police reports, the pair were under investigation for interstate drug trafficking in 1991. Among the associates was James Marks, a low-level hood, who was shot to death outside his apartment in Lynn, Massachusetts, in February 1991. Marks must have picked up some information about the Gardner case before he was killed, as he told his girlfriend at the time that he had hidden some valuable stolen items in the space above their ceiling. Nearly twenty years later, in 2010, that information was relayed to the FBI, which searched the crawl space—without success.

Berghman decided that the best thing for him to do was to seek legal advice, and he contacted Bernard Grossberg, a Boston lawyer who had ably represented his son in a criminal case. The three of them—Grossberg, Jeanine Guarente, Guarente's daughter from an earlier marriage, and Berghman—reached a deal: If Guarente was able to find out what had happened to the paintings, then the three of them would split whatever reward money was forthcoming.

From the outset, Grossberg was enthused by the prospect of a recovery, and he already had reason to suspect a connection between Guarente and the Gardner masterpieces. Grossberg had represented one of the four defendants in a federal criminal case that had just been completed, and Guarente's name had come up several times in the FBI files as being a possible link to the paintings.

"We need tangible proof to convince the museum and the FBI that what you're saying is a legitimate lead," Grossberg stressed to Berghman and Jeanine Guarente. "You've got to come up with concrete evidence."

Twice in a matter of months Jeanine produced what she claimed were chips she had collected from paintings her late father had at their home in Madison, Maine. Twice Grossberg presented them to Arnold Hiatt, a trustee for the Gardner Museum who had worked tirelessly to recover the paintings. But on both occasions the chips turned out to be fakes. In fact, the second batch turned out to have come from the edges of a magazine that someone had snipped off.

"I was very hopeful about this when the chips came," Grossberg said. "Unfortunately, testing proved them otherwise, so all those hopes evaporated."

The episode involving Guarente's daughter and Berghman—and the phony chips—was never made known to the FBI. In fact, both Grossberg and Berghman told me the FBI never questioned them regarding their interactions. And Hiatt says he thought so little of what they had to offer that he never passed on the information to the FBI or the museum's key investigator, Anthony Amore. Yet eight years later, the FBI was strongly suggesting that Guarente had been a central player in the stashing of the artwork

---

ELENE GUARENTE was having a hard time financially after Robert's death. The Italian restaurant she had opened near her home in Madison, Maine, had closed and she was living on Social Security disability assistance. She had lost more than fifty pounds, she says from the stress, and on top of it all her car had broken down and it needed at least $1,000 in repairs.

Still, while she admits she needed money desperately, Elene denies she summoned the feds. Instead she is adamant that in March 2010, the FBI reached out to her, telling Elene that they wanted to talk to her about the Gardner heist and the missing paintings.

She wouldn't talk. Instead she reached out to Robert Gentile.

Gentile was her late husband's good friend. Guarente had told her Gentile would look after her if anything ever happened to her. She knew he would honor that.

"Bobby, I'm in need of money," she began. "I know my husband gave you those stolen paintings. You need to come to Maine to talk to Earle Berghman. He's my soul mate. You two need to sort this out. If you don't come, I'm calling back the feds."

"I don't know what you're talking about," Gentile told her. "But I'll come." She was his old friend's wife and he felt it was the right thing to do.

Berghman and Gentile met in a food court at a Portland mall. It was April 2010. Berghman didn't beat around the bush. He looked Gentile right in the eye and told him, "I know Bobby gave you those paintings."

"I don't know what you're talking about," Gentile shot back.

Berghman thought he was lying. Maybe this was what happened to the paintings that Guarente's daughter told him five years earlier she had seen hanging in her father's house—he had given them to Gentile. Gentile kept his head down as he denied Berghman's accusations. He wouldn't look him in the eye. Instead, he told Berghman that if Elene needed money, why didn't she call the Boston lawyer who had provided her late husband with a $30,000 loan in the late 1980s that he used to buy his first house in central Maine. Maybe he could help Elene out now, Gentile said he told Berghman.

And, Gentile told me, there was another reason he remembered the lawyer—Guarente had mentioned the lawyer's name to him in relationship to the Gardner paintings years before, and that Gentile thought the reference was serious enough that he passed the information on to the FBI.

He was right. Sometime in early 2010, Elene Guarente had summoned the FBI's Geoff Kelly and Anthony Amore, security chief for the Gardner, to her Maine home and was relaying her suspicions about her late husband, Gentile, and the stolen Gardner paintings.

This is what she told them: In the early 1990s, her husband showed her a painting shortly after they moved into the "white farmhouse" in Madison, Maine. They never spoke about the paintings again until 2002 or 2003, when her husband, who was then sick with cancer, told her they were taking a drive to

Portland to have lunch with his old friend Bobby Gentile and his wife, she said.

On their way home from the lunch, Elene told the investigators, Guarente had told her he had given three paintings to Gentile for safekeeping in Connecticut.

"My Bobby was sick then," she recalled later. "He told me he wanted them left with someone who'd make sure they were safe and would be able to provide for me. He thought he could trust Bobby Gentile with that job. The next year my Bobby died and I never heard anything about it after that."

"That's ridiculous," Gentile practically spits back when told of the tale Elene Guarente shared. "I remember that lunch. But not because Guarente handed off any paintings to me. That's crazy. He didn't. What I remember most was that Elene ordered the twin lobsters. Two of them! And we were only having lunch!"

CHAPTER EIGHT

HOLLYWOOD HANDSOME

ELENE GUARENTE wasn't the only one reaching out to Robert Gentile in recent years, asking for his assistance in recovering the stolen Gardner artwork. David Turner, who had been suspected from the earliest days of being involved in the 1990 heist, was doing the same thing from his prison cell in New York.

In November 2010, several months after first being contacted by Elene, Gentile received a letter from Turner, who was serving a thirty-year sentence in federal prison for trying to rob an armored car headquarters, reminding him that they had known each other through Guarente. Turner was hoping to help in the recovery of the Gardner paintings and asked Gentile if he would be willing to help him out by calling a former girlfriend of Turner's who was now living in Boston.

Initially, Gentile says, his gut told him to steer clear. But he was in a bind with the feds, trying to maneuver his way out of the bust for selling prescription drugs, and he knew that helping to recover the Gardner pieces might just be his get-out-of-jail-free card.

So when Geoff Kelly, the special agent in charge of the Gardner investigation, asked Gentile to call the girlfriend as a favor to the FBI, he decided right away that it couldn't hurt his chances. Gentile was beginning to see the possibility that providing information or assistance that provided the federal agents with a lead to the recovery of the stolen artwork might also put him in line to collect some of the $5 million in reward money the museum had long made available. If dealing with Turner was part of what he needed to go through to help the feds recover the paintings, then so be it.

After a day or two of exchanging messages, Gentile finally spoke to the woman, in a phone call that was taped by federal agents. The girlfriend told Gentile that Turner wanted him to meet with two of his old friends from Boston, both ex-convicts with long prison records.

Gentile knew one of the two, Richard Gillis, who like Turner had long been associated with the Rossetti crime gang out of East Boston. Gillis was known as a tough guy. In fact, he'd survived being wounded twice in gunfights, the last in 1994.

Gentile thanked her for the phone call and said he would call her back to set up the meeting.

Kelly pressed Gentile to agree to the meeting, even suggesting that an agent accompany him. The agent, of course, would serve two purposes: He'd offer protection for Gentile, but he'd also try to make his own ties to the ex-convicts.

"You want me to help you put someone on the inside of a gang in Boston?" Gentile said to Kelly, balking. "I don't want to have anything more to do with any of this."

Gentile walked out of the room and stopped cooperating with the FBI from that point on.

DAVID A. TURNER was so good-looking as a young man that his lawyer referred to him as "Hollywood." But Turner was also extraordinarily reckless and manipulative, so much so that he had an affair with the lawyer's daughter-in-law, causing her to lose her husband and Turner to lose his lawyer. It was an unfortunate turn of events because Turner was starting to get into serious trouble.

By the summer that he graduated from high school, police were questioning Turner and his best friend about the murder of a social worker who was unlucky enough to offer them a lift from Provincetown to their home ninety miles away. A few years later, it was Turner's best friend who was murdered, and Turner himself was the prime suspect. Charles "Chewie" Pappas had been spilling to the Massachusetts state police about some of Turner's criminal exploits and was about to take the stand against Turner when he was shot to death.

But to those who grew up with him, Turner was anything but an evil kid. He was a standout on the football and ski teams, dated the beautiful daughter of the town's most prestigious political leader, and liked hanging out with friends at Sunset Lake, sipping beers and listening to The Clash deep into the night. Sure, he liked to raise a little hell—as evidenced by the quotes he left behind on his 1985 Braintree High School yearbook, "Better to burn out, than to fade away," read one, from a Neil Young song; the other from Billy Joel, "Only the good die young"—but that wasn't so unusual.

Turner lost his father at thirteen, and sometime in the mid-1980s, before he had even graduated from high school, he met and fell under the influence of Robert Guarente, the old bank robber and mobster with ties to organized crime figures throughout greater Boston. It was a perfect match: Guarente liked how tough and aggressive Turner was—he soon began referring to Turner as "my kid"—and Turner liked how close Guarente was with serious mobsters.

Turner has emerged as a key figure in the FBI's connect-the-dots account of what happened to the Gardner masterpieces, and perhaps the architect of the actual theft. But the details of his ties to the heist are even more tenuous than those of Guarente and Gentile.

Turner has steadfastly denied that he has any knowledge about the theft, and continues to say he is not writing a book about his role in it, as it has been reported he is doing. He also swears that he isn't cooperating with the FBI in trying to figure out what happened to the stolen paintings, and that he was misquoted by an author who reported that Turner told him he should be on the cover of his book on the Gardner case.

Despite those denials, the FBI has suspected almost from the start that Turner played a role in the Gardner theft, and that he was in fact one of the two men disguised as Boston police officers who carried out the heist. Agents even went so far as to send his fingerprints to the FBI's lab in Quantico, Virginia, in the early aftermath of the heist but failed to come up with any match.

———————————

BOBBY GUARENTE always told David Turner to keep his plans and exploits to himself and Turner took it to heart. As a result Guarente trusted him and wouldn't have thought twice about telling Turner how vulnerable the Gardner Museum was to theft, something Guarente would have learned from his family ties to Stephen and Ralph Rossetti, major figures in an East Boston crime gang. The Rossettis in turn had plotted a Gardner break-in with Louis Royce from as far back as the early 1980s.

Remarkably, Massachusetts state police had Turner under surveillance during the months leading up to and just after the Gardner theft. But the crime they were investigating him for had nothing to do with art theft. Instead, Turner was being watched in connection with his suspected involvement in a widespread cocaine distribution network operating out of an auto repair garage shop in Dorchester operated by Carmello Merlino, a low-level mobster.

The surveillance, which lasted between 1989 and 1991, centered on the Dorchester shop and the handful of people, including Turner, who were implicated. On several occasions the police even tracked Turner's travels.

Under customary procedure, such an operation would have been a joint federal-state investigation, which would have brought more agents into the probe, and undoubtedly more surveillance of Turner and its other principal targets.

But this investigation had been funded by a separate grant to the Massachusetts attorney general's office, and involved only Massachusetts state police and local police officers, so there was no coordination with agents from the FBI or Drug Enforcement Administration. Might a greater surveillance force have prevented the Gardner heist by interrupting the conspirators in their planning stage, or even as it was being carried out? We can only speculate.

The surveillance, even though it was conducted randomly according to the availability of officers assigned to the trafficking case, produced several major coups, such as the recovery of the pizza box used for a cocaine delivery, and provided the physical evidence needed to indict both Merlino and Turner's high school friend Charles Pappas, who later wound up shot.

It also led to a rare miss: Officers on surveillance during the sting observed Turner as he carried a "Chinese vase" into the Boston office of a lawyer just eighteen months after the Gardner theft. Turner was not stopped and questioned about the vase, but a Chinese "beaker" was among the thirteen items stolen from the museum. Alfred A. Sollitto, the Boston lawyer, later said in an interview that Turner, whom he knew socially, often brought him antiques he thought Sollitto might be interested in buying. But that day he had no interest in the vase and Turner took it away. He said he couldn't recall what the vase Turner showed to him looked like, but doubted it was anything valuable or had come from the Gardner heist.

The surveillance had been authorized by a Massachusetts judge on the basis of a sixty-four-page affidavit submitted by a state police officer summarizing the investigation into the cocaine ring. A confidential informant was quoted in the affidavit as stating that Pappas, Turner, and a third associate were "involved in the distribution of controlled substances and that (the informant) in 1989 was present with Pappas and Turner while they were in possession of what Turner and Pappas stated . . . was a kilogram of cocaine."

The affidavit then quoted Turner as telling the informant he was going to drive his Corvette to Florida in March 1990—the month the Gardner theft occurred—"to pick up a large amount of cocaine and (return) to Massachusetts with the controlled substance."

Perhaps Turner was using his involvement in the cocaine trafficking network to divert investigators' attention from his involvement in the Gardner heist, or perhaps he was involved in both schemes. The affidavit provides some tantalizing—if conflicting—clues.

After hearing from his source that Turner was on a cocaine run to Florida, a detective involved in the investigation called Turner's residence in early March 1990, days before the Gardner theft, and asked for him. A woman answered the phone and said that Turner "was on a mini vacation in Florida."

While there, according to other investigative documents, Turner used his American Express credit card to pay for $645 worth of merchandise from a "Spy Shops" store in Miami Beach. Although there is no inventory as to what Turner

David A. Turner, now serving a long federal prison sentence for participating in an attempted armored car heist, has long been rumored to have been involved in the Gardner theft. A good friend recently said that Turner was writing a book about the case, but Turner denied that as well as any role in the heist.

bought, the store, according to its advertisements at the time, specialized in electronic equipment that could monitor police calls as well as conduct surveillance or determine if a person was being targeted for surveillance.

That purchase was made on March 15, 1990, and the receipt shows Turner's signature. The Gardner theft would take place 1,500 miles away and less than three days later in Boston.

Turner's credit card was next used on March 20—two days after the theft—at Dollar Rent-A-Car in Fort Lauderdale to pay the $530.94 charge for a rental car. Again, Turner's signature was used to sign the credit card voucher, though it also contained another person's Social Security number, which investigators say suggests someone other than Turner might have been using his credit card that day. I was unable to trace the Social Security number written on the receipt.

Regardless, it is certain that Turner was back in Boston at least a few days after the robbery. Public records show he appeared at a 9 A.M. hearing at Quincy District Court, near his

Braintree home, and pleaded guilty to a misdemeanor charge of driving while his license had been suspended three years before. He paid a fine and left the courthouse.

Certainly the composite drawing of one of the two thieves bears a strong resemblance to Turner, with his cocky smile and the mischievous cast in his right eye. The museum's night watchman, who spent the longest time with the two thieves and helped draw up the composites later, told me in 2013 that Turner did look like one of the pair.

While Turner denies he had anything to do with the theft, sources familiar with the FBI investigation confirm that Des-Lauriers had him in mind when he made the startling 2013 announcement that the FBI knew who had carried out the theft. Also, while Turner denied that he is writing a book about the theft, a close friend gushed about it as recently as 2013.

"David's decided to go ahead and write his story," said Chris Ruggiero, Turner's longtime friend who speaks to him frequently on the phone. "He's going to reach out to [actor] Mark Wahlberg's company to see if they want to get an option on it." Wahlberg grew up in Boston.

It would take a Wahlberg-like script to capture Turner's life, including repeated criminal offenses that, even when he was apprehended, rarely resulted in serious punishment. And in no period was he so criminally active as the months before and following the Gardner theft, raising again the questions of why and how he would have been involved in other robberies if he had just pulled off the largest single art theft in world history.

IN JANUARY 1990, Turner and another man drove up to a suburban home in Canton, outside of Boston, where they had heard the owner kept sizable amounts of cash. Dressed as a deliveryman, Turner rang the doorbell and burst into the foyer when a woman opened the door. After first holding a gun to her head and then tying her up with masking tape, Turner and his accomplice robbed the house of $130,000 in cash and jewelry.

Then, two months after the Gardner heist, on May 18, 1990, Turner, Pappas, and a third gangster, Leonard DiMuzio, were arrested after breaking into a home in Tewksbury, a small town north of Boston. Even though the charges included possession of a handgun, and DiMuzio admitted the three were involved in the theft, Turner was sentenced to only sixty days in prison.

Although they got off practically scot-free after their arrest, the trio never worked again, and in March 1991 DiMuzio disappeared after visiting his sister in the hospital. Several months later his body was found, stuffed into the trunk of his car, dead from multiple gunshots to the head.

Police were without clues in both the Canton robbery and DiMuzio's murder until April 1992, when state police arrested Merlino and Pappas—but not Turner—for cocaine trafficking. With past criminal records, both Pappas and Merlino realized they faced serious time if they were convicted, so they decided to cooperate with investigators.

"I am in fear of my life and the lives of my family," Pappas wrote in an August 1992 note to Edward Whelan, a state police officer with whom he had prior dealings and held in high regard.

"Turner and DiMuzio pulled that Canton home invasion," Pappas told Whelan when they finally met. "They pulled the heist at Cheers, too."

Whelan was shocked. The September 1991 robbery at Cheers, Boston's iconic pub, had been front-page news but had remained unsolved. But the best was yet to come from Pappas.

"Turner shot DiMuzio," he finally said to the trooper. "He was angry that DiMuzio had given the cops details of his part in the Tewksbury break-in, but most of all because he'd held out on his share of the money stolen in the job."

Although Pappas outlined a laundry list of offenses, he made no mention of Turner being involved in planning or carrying out the Gardner Museum theft.

Merlino was trying another avenue to avoid going to jail on the 1992 cocaine trafficking charges. Through a lawyer, he reached out to Turner to try to recover the stolen Gardner paintings. The lawyer, who asked not to be identified, said he believed the authorities would be willing to drop the charges against Merlino if he could deliver the stolen artwork.

Turner promised to try. But days later, he called the lawyer back. "I was close but someone got spooked," Turner said. "The best I can tell you is that they were in the basement of a church in South Boston."

There were nearly a dozen churches within South Boston's borders. Searches turned up nothing and Merlino was stuck, left to serve a short sentence in state prison on the cocaine trafficking charges.

Pappas, whose father had been shot to death in a gangland shooting in 1981, suffered a far worse fate than Merlino. In November 1995, less than a month before he was to testify against his old buddy Turner on the home invasion, Pappas walked into the home of his girlfriend's parents with his arms filled with grocery bags for Thanksgiving dinner.

Two men burst into the breezeway of the house just as he got there. Their faces were covered with ski masks and they fired eight bullets into Pappas, including two into his mouth. Screaming, his girlfriend called Braintree police, who found Pappas still alive but with blood everywhere.

"I didn't see who did it," Pappas told them, his speech garbled from the blood in his mouth. Gasping for air, he said, "There were two guys."

Pappas's girlfriend was in hysterics, and she said to the cops, "He told me David Turner did this to him."

"How do you know it was Turner, Charlie?" Braintree police sergeant Karen MacAleese asked Pappas.

"I know he did this because I'm testifying against him next week."

EMTs were swarming around, and they rushed Pappas into a waiting ambulance. Lieutenant Paul Frasier, who had known Pappas from his many prior scrapes with the law, jumped in.

"Who did this to you, Charlie?" Frasier asked him.

Pappas opened his eyes and recognized Frasier.

"Go fuck yourself," he hissed, and closed his eyes for the final time. He was dead before they reached the hospital.

Just a few hours later, Turner, looking sharp in fresh clothes, was approached in front of his home by several Braintree police officers who told him they wanted to talk to him about Pappas's killing.

"If you've got any questions for me I'm willing to hear you out, but you've gotta call Martin Leppo first." This was probably the first that the Braintree police knew that Leppo, a well-known criminal defense lawyer in the area, represented Turner. Turner could now be added to at least a half dozen individuals such as Robert Guarente, Stephen Rossetti, Myles Connor, Louis Royce, Dicky Joyce, and William Youngworth, whom Leppo represented who were considered suspects or at least having information on the Gardner theft at one time or another. "If we have any questions for you, we'll find you on our own, don't worry," one of the officers responded.

THE SHOOTING OF A PROSPECTIVE WITNESS in a criminal trial sent shock waves through Massachusetts law enforcement. Massachusetts Governor William Weld, who had been a US attorney and head of the Justice Department's Criminal Division, decried the lack of state resources to adequately protect such witnesses.

With the principal witness dead, Martin Leppo pressed to have Turner's trial go forward. But if Pappas's death wasn't enough, at the next court hearing state prosecutors revealed that another key witness, the woman who had been held captive at gunpoint while the Canton home was ransacked, was too afraid to testify. To top it off, a state police captain testified that Turner's friends had approached her boyfriend at a nearby mall and threatened to kill him if she testified.

"He was very scared," she said. "He had no doubt if I testified he would be killed."

She never did, and the charges were soon dropped. Turner, who had denied the charges that he was responsible for the home invasion, had again beaten the rap and was set free. The furor soon died down and, as with his father before him, no one was ever prosecuted for Charles Pappas's murder.

But the heat brought down on Turner from these repeated close encounters with the law had an effect all the same. After the charges were dropped in 1995, Turner went straight.

Besides, the mob had figured out that there was a new way in Boston to make huge amounts of money, quickly and legally: through contracts related to the Big Dig.

Originally predicted to cost the federal government $2.8 billion, the Big Dig was a major construction project intended to place underground the major artery that cuts through the center of Boston, and build a new tunnel to Logan Airport beneath Boston Harbor. Due to unforeseen problems and delays, the project's budget was ballooning to $14.6 billion. Turner and Stevie Rossetti, his mobster friend from East Boston who had served prison time for bank robbery and conspiracy, decided to get in on the bonanza. Both established trucking companies and during the mid-1990s landed more than $20 million in contracts from the state Department of Transportation.

But even with all that money on the table, the chance of making millions through a quick and dirty score had too much appeal for both men.

Carmello Merlino, having served his time for cocaine trafficking, was working on a new criminal opportunity out of his Dorchester radiator shop. A parolee named Anthony Romano Jr. who had come to work for his repair shop said an armored car headquarters in nearby Easton was ripe for hitting. Romano had a friend who was a guard on the inside and was in total control of the headquarters on Sunday mornings. There was as much as $50 million ready for the taking, he assured Merlino.

But Anthony Romano Jr. didn't happen to secure his job at Merlino's shop by accident. He had been placed there by an FBI agent, David Nadolski, after he'd assisted Nadolski in recovering three priceless Bibles and a fourth book stolen from the Adams National Historic Site in Quincy. It wasn't long before Romano reported back that Merlino was discussing the Gardner Museum paintings, and his interest in recovering them.

Merlino wasn't interested in their value; rather, he wanted to gain the release of someone out of jail this time. The $5 million reward that the Gardner was offering for information that led to the recovery of the artwork was just icing on the cake.

The talk about the Gardner case became so frequent that Merlino didn't blink when two FBI agents, including Neil Cronin, who was assigned to the Gardner recovery case, showed up repeatedly in 1998 to remind him of the agency's interest in getting the stolen masterpieces back.

After one of the meetings with the FBI agents, Merlino told Romano that if the deal went awry for any reason, the younger man would be suspected as the weak link and Merlino would make sure Turner killed Romano as well as his daughter.

An air of inevitability hung over the garage that Merlino could facilitate the paintings' return. So strong was this perceived probability that Cronin's supervisor in the FBI's Boston office visited Anne Hawley, still the Gardner's director, in September 1998 with some good news: The FBI now knew who had stolen the paintings, FBI supervisor W. Thomas Cassano told Hawley. While he didn't provide any names, her notes of their conversation quote Cassano as saying, "One is in jail, one is on the street, and one is dead."

Reports quickly spread among the trustees that the thief who had died had suffered a drug overdose soon after the theft. The one in jail was actually also thought to be dead, killed by members of the mid-Atlantic mob of which he was a low-level member. Little was known of the third individual, the one who was still on the streets, except that he had masterminded the theft.

In the ensuing years, the thief who died of a drug overdose has been rumored to be George Reissfelder, a low-level hood who'd migrated into Merlino's gang in the 1980s after being released from prison—with the help of legal representation by John F. Kerry, before he became US senator from Massachusetts and Democratic nominee for president—for a murder and robbery he was later absolved of.

No clues to the Gardner robbery were found after a search of Reissfelder's apartment, but his brother and sister later told investigators that they recalled seeing a painting that looked much like the Edouard Manet *Chez Tortoni* hanging in his bedroom. The painting had been banged out of its frame when stolen from the Gardner, and Reissfelder had hung the painting in his bedroom in a new frame.

"I may not be able to tell you if a painting hung in a museum or was bought at Wal-Mart, but I could tell that one in George's room was something beautiful," says his sister, Donna Reissfelder Mauras, who now lives in Tucson, Arizona. "But I told George that the frame he had the painting in didn't fit at all. It was a golden frame, too frou-frou, for a painting of a man like that one was."

There were several other clues that drew investigators to look at Reissfelder. Chief among them was his face: Long, narrow, and more youthful-looking than his age of forty, Reissfelder looked like the older of the two thieves in the police sketches. Also, Reissfelder and Turner were friends, having hung out together at Merlino's Dorchester auto-repair shop. Robert Beauchamp, who met Reissfelder while serving time in Massachusetts state prisons, said Reissfelder and Turner visited him several times in prison in the eighteen months after the Gardner robbery and before Reissfelder died in July 1991.

"George wouldn't tell me what it was, but when he came by himself, he did say he had done something with Turner," Beauchamp said.

Although the Massachusetts Department of Correction refuses to release records of the visits, investigators confirm Beauchamp's account that Reissfelder and Turner visited him together.

While the case implicating Reissfelder in the Gardner robbery is circumstantial at best, the information on him that Beauchamp and Reissfelder's relatives gave investigators was sufficient to get a few warrants. On that basis they conducted complete searches of three of the houses he or his relatives lived in, but found nothing.

There's no doubt, though, that what Reissfelder had in his possession was important to Merlino, whose automotive repair shop Reissfelder visited often in the months before his death. The morning he was found dead in his apartment building, it was Merlino and an associate who summoned the

Quincy Fire Department when they were unable to gain entry to the unit on their own. Maybe it was to buy cocaine to feed his growing addiction that drew Reissfelder to Merlino's garage, or maybe it was to meet with other cronies including Turner, Pappas, and Guarente, whom law enforcement often found there and whose names have been associated with the Gardner theft, but many answers died with Reissfelder when he overdosed that summer day.

MERLINO'S FOUR-YEAR SENTENCE in state prison for cocaine trafficking out of his garage didn't stop his strategizing on how to get his hands on the stolen masterpieces.

An FBI investigative report written July 21, 1998, quoted Romano, its undercover informant, as telling the agents that Merlino had told him he had seven of the Gardner paintings and was working out a deal with criminal defense lawyer Martin Leppo to have them returned to the museum. Leppo was drawing up a plan, according to Merlino, that would ensure immunity from prosecution for possessing stolen property as well as an equitable plan to divide up the $5 million reward the museum was offering.

At least $1 million would go to Youngworth, which was only fair considering he would have been instrumental in getting the artwork returned. According to Merlino, Youngworth had the paintings after Myles Connor, who was off to serve a ten-year sentence in federal prison, placed them in his safekeeping.

Although Youngworth had backed out of a deal with the FBI to return the paintings himself, Merlino figured he had a way of convincing Youngworth to give up the artwork to him. He was going to kidnap Youngworth's young son and hold him hostage until Youngworth, then in prison, decided to deal with him.

As this plan suggests, Merlino was becoming more and more desperate in trying to find ways to recover the paintings, and at the same time becoming more and more suspicious of the FBI. He refused to have any conversations on the phone or inside the garage, fearing it was bugged, and believing the agents had hired lip readers to decipher his conversations when he was outside.

The only person Merlino seemed to trust was Richard Chicofsky, a well-known FBI informant and local scam artist who prided himself on dealing with criminal associates and their lawyers, as well as federal investigators and prosecutors. In late 1997, over a two-day period, Romano watched as Merlino had conversations about the missing Gardner paintings with Chicofsky, Turner, Guarente, and Leppo.

"Those Gardner paintings are coming up more and more," Romano told David Nadolski, his FBI handler, on New Year's Eve 1997. "I think this Chicofsky guy is the man in charge. He's going to get them back for Merlino."

Since he was focused on Merlino's interest in striking the armored car headquarters, Nadolski brought the information to Neil Cronin, the FBI's lead agent on the Gardner theft at the time. Within days, Cronin and Nadolski arranged to meet privately with Chicofsky at the cafeteria of a Veterans Affairs clinic in Boston.

Everyone knew Chicofsky as "Fat Richie." He weighed close to three hundred pounds but, like TV star Jackie Gleason a generation before, he maintained an air of sophistication with a preference for silk suits and men's cologne.

"Richie, we hear you're talking about the stolen Gardner paintings with Carmello Merlino," Cronin said to him.

"I might be able to do something for you there," Chicofsky told the agents. "But I need to know if you'll come through for me, if I do this for you."

He went on to explain that he had become friends with a Chinese woman who might be facing deportation over an expired visa.

"You help me, and I might be able to help you with those paintings," Chicofsky said.

"You mean you might have access to the paintings?" Nadolski asked him directly.

"Not me," Chicofsky said. "Merlino is giving me hints that he's able to get his hands on them."

Chicofsky asked the agents to go along with a scheme. He wanted to play along with Merlino and his plans for recovering the paintings but then trick him so that Chicofsky wound up with the paintings. That way he, and not Merlino, would get the $5 million reward.

Confused, Nadolski went back to Romano and asked him, "Tell me again, what's the relationship between these two guys? Who's got the paintings, Merlino or Chicofsky?"

Romano said it wasn't clear to him but his gut told him that it was Merlino who held the upper hand and Chicofsky was trying to con his way into Merlino's good graces. Cronin went back to Merlino and pressed him—did he have the paintings or not? Merlino said he didn't have them within reach but was working to locate them.

On being debriefed by Cronin, Nadolski shook his head in disbelief that the two aging con men were now trying to con each other over the missing Gardner paintings. He was glad he was not the case agent in the 1990 robbery, but instead was concentrating on the more straightforward matter of Merlino's plans for hitting the armored car headquarters.

But having Romano agree to assist him in doing whatever it took to infiltrate—and bring down—Merlino's operation gave Nadolski an enviable weapon. If Romano, with his nervous manner and skinny arms marked with heroin tracks, was the picture of an ex-convict, then Nadolski, with a friendly demeanor and a no-nonsense professionalism, was the epitome of a federal agent. He had been in the FBI for more than ten years and was known for his ability to gain the confidence of informants.

A bond of friendship and trust slowly grew between them and for much of 1998 Romano, playing the role of the loser kid inside the Dorchester auto body shop Merlino used as the center of his criminal operations, reported back to Nadolski what he saw and heard going on there.

Totally unaware that Romano was working as an informant for the FBI, Merlino trusted him more and more. He pressed him on whether he knew anyone without a criminal record who might be able to land a guard's job at the Loomis-Fargo armored car headquarters in Easton. Once the friend had landed the job, Merlino said, he could put together a crew to rob the place of the $50 million he believed was held there during weekends.

The friend Romano found for the job was in fact an undercover agent the FBI had made ready for the role. He was prepared to start working at Loomis-Fargo and then slowly earn Merlino's trust. Nadolski told Romano that the only way they could go forward to target Merlino's scheme was if Romano agreed to play a bigger role, and wear a wire to secretly record his conversations with Merlino. According to an unpublished memoir Romano later wrote, Nadolski had been able to win over his trust by being honest with him about the perils of what they were doing and how he would be protected. But the prospect of a new life in the federal witness protection program also appealed to him.

"How many chances had I been given by my own father and messed up?" he wrote. "Dave thought a fresh start would appeal to me, and he was right. I loved the idea from the start."

Nadolski had his goal for the operation: If it worked, it would mean the two of them—the G-man and the ex-con who had been a lifelong heroin addict—would be responsible for the biggest undercover success in the history of the Boston FBI office.

Merlino began talking about the armored car score almost from the time Romano went to work for his auto body shop in late 1997. He soon drafted his nephew Billy into the plan, but still several more were needed to carry out the score. For the next year, Romano, who never graduated from high school and battled drug addiction for his entire life, tried to keep the FBI informed of what was going at Merlino's auto body shop, and the two biggest investigations being tracked inside it: the missing Gardner paintings and planning of a $50 million armored car heist.

The two cases came together in early 1999. Merlino put together the five members of the crew to carry out the robbery of the armored car headquarters—including "Hollywood" David Turner and Stephen Rossetti.

The FBI agents had gotten word from Romano the night before that the group was going ahead with the robbery plans. With Romano wearing the wire that secretly taped the conversation, the group had met at a pancake house a short distance from Merlino's garage to go over the final details.

Merlino was worried about the guards. "Just supposing whatever fuckin' freaky thing happened that these two motherfuckers or one of them can get up," he blustered.

"He's not gonna get up," Rossetti said. "I'll make sure these guys are secured."

The guards, it was promised, would be tied with nooses that would tighten if they moved.

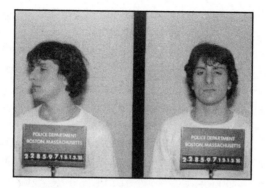

An active member of his uncle's East Boston criminal gang, Stephen Rossetti was involved in armed robberies in the Greater Boston area in the 1970s and 1980s.

Turner said little, allowing Merlino and Rossetti to carry on about how they were ready to handle any surprise. Turner worried that if the police saw him and Merlino together, they might suspect they were up to something sinister. And he worried about the score itself. When robberies are under way, "a half hour feels like three hours," Turner said. But he said he was ready if the need came to "throw down" with any police who tried to stop him.

Rossetti made up in bluster what Turner may have lacked. At one point, a night or two before the theft was to take place, Rossetti and Romano sat together in the back of Merlino's garage in a van that would be used in the robbery, going over the final details of the roles each would play.

"Steve Rossetti so loves himself and his criminal prowess, the dude is off his chain," Romano wrote later of the encounter. "The quiet, up and coming wiseguy, closely connected to New England mob boss Cadillac Frank Salemme, Steve could not shut up! Him and I were bonding back there in the mini-van."

Rossetti's big concern was about the weapons he and Turner would be bringing to the heist—"equipment," he called it. Included in the arsenal was a Ruger Mini-14 semiautomatic rifle. At one point, in showing Romano how he would carry the rifle into the armored car headquarters, Rossetti put his hands on Romano's lower stomach, in the exact same place he was usually wearing his tape recorder.

Luckily, he wasn't wearing it that night.

"I was well aware that after all the recording I had done, all the meetings and phone calls with the feds, all the dry runs to Easton (the location of the warehouse), the whole investigation and probably my next birthday would have gone up in smoke if I had that recorder on me," Romano wrote.

Turner focused on the details of the robbery and how it would proceed. There would be three vehicles—Merlino alone in a getaway car; Billy, his nephew, driving the van laden with the weapons and with Turner and Rossetti in the back; and Romano in his own van, which on the sign from his friend, the guard on the inside, he would drive inside the warehouse and fill with $50 million.

Eerily similar to the two "police officers" who had pulled off the Gardner Museum heist nine years before, Turner and Rossetti carried walkie-talkies and communicated with each other only through them. Also, Turner reminded the crew that once the theft was completed, they needed to make certain they found the device that captured their entry into the building and robbery, and, as took place at the end of the Gardner theft, took the recorded tape with them.

The morning before the robbery was to take place, Turner showed up at the garage to tell Merlino that he was "very excited" about the next day and that everything looked good. He then handed Romano a cell phone wrapped in a rag.

"Give this to your inside guy this afternoon," he told Romano. "He's to use this to call you tomorrow morning, to tell you everything's okay on his end and we should do this."

The crew would be waiting nearby in their three separate vehicles.

The day would begin with Turner driving his own car, a Chevy Tahoe, and meeting Rossetti before dawn so they could assemble the weapons. Then they would proceed together to Merlino's garage in Dorchester in Rossetti's smaller Honda. There they would load everything in one of the two vans.

The garage lot was empty when they first drove by. Concerned that they might be stopped driving a car loaded with weapons as they continued to search for Merlino, Rossetti and Turner drove back to Turner's Tahoe and transferred the guns into it. An FBI search of the vehicle later turned up five fully loaded semiautomatic handguns, and the Ruger Mini-14 semiautomatic rifle, fully loaded as well. Tucked in with all the weaponry were bulletproof vests, police scanners, masking tape, Halloween masks, and an explosive-fragmentation hand grenade.

Under federal law, presence of such an explosive during the commission of a crime allows a judge to increase by twice as much if not more the number of years on a prison sentence.

After dumping the weapons, the two men were unarmed as they continued to zip up and down Dorchester's backstreets in Rossetti's red Honda in a desperate search for the other members of their crew. They were totally unaware that Merlino and his nephew had already been arrested by Federal agents when they arrived at the garage earlier, and totally unaware that their every turn was being tracked by a surveillance team that included two agents in a small plane flying overhead.

They were close to abandoning their plan as they drove onto Morrissey Boulevard and neared a public skating rink that was quickly filling with fathers bringing their kids to morning hockey practice. Out of nowhere, two GMC Suburbans smashed into the Honda, running it onto the side of the road. Agents surrounded the vehicle and Turner and Rossetti surrendered without a fight.

The pair were quickly taken under armed guard to the Brookline police station and placed in separate cells. Among the first people to approach them in their cells was FBI agent Neil Cronin. He reminded Turner that no one had gotten hurt and that no guns had been fired in the day's adventure. Everything could be forgotten if he helped recover the Gardner paintings, Cronin said.

As Turner would later write to another author, the FBI was convinced that he had a hand in the museum robbery and getting his cooperation to recover the missing artwork was at the center of the FBI's decision to allow the plot to rob the armored car headquarters to proceed.

"They think that I was the person who committed the (museum) robbery, which is false," said Turner in the letter. "They thought that if I was facing serious charges, I would be motivated to help facilitate the return of the paintings. Well, they got the serious charges against me, and now I am going to die in prison."

Rossetti, too, was worried about what a long prison sentence might mean for him and, before the trial took place, he got word to Turner asking for a significant favor: Would Turner acknowledge in court that it was his idea to bring an arsenal of weapons, especially the hand grenade? Rossetti faced a longer sentence than the others because he had already been convicted of a bank robbery, and had served a long prison sentence for it. He had a wife and son now, and did not want to serve the rest of his life in jail.

Turner made no such admission during the trial and Rossetti was correct that his past conviction would bring a heavier sentence. In 2002, after the entire crew was convicted of robbery and conspiracy charges, Rossetti was sentenced to more than fifty-three years in federal prison. Turner was sentenced to thirty-eight years. Both sentences were longer by thirty years because of the hand grenade they'd brought.

But Turner was not done with the courts. He spent the next five years appealing to either have his conviction overturned or be granted a new trial. His principal argument was still that the government had entrapped him into joining the robbery scheme to force him to provide information on the missing Gardner paintings.

The appeals court upheld his conviction and denied his request for a new trial in August 2007. In its twenty-seven-page opinion, the court found that his two prior convictions involving weapons possession and robbery, in 1989 and 1990, and his deep ties to Merlino cast a shadow on his claim he was a total innocent to the robbery scheme.

Evidence at his trial showed that Turner had been sufficiently involved in planning the robbery, including casing the headquarters to make sure the insider was cooperating, to nullify the argument that he had been coerced into the scheme.

"Turner engaged in additional surveillance of the target, ran an additional dry run with the 'insider,' stated that the group should shoot it out with police if stopped, expressed concern that his Tahoe was bugged, commiserated with Rosetti [sic] about the intense impatience one feels while waiting to begin a planned robbery, and expressed concern that he and Merlino should not be seen together because people know that when they are together something illegal is going to happen," wrote Appeals Court Justice Jeffrey R. Howard.

It must have been a rude awakening for Turner. But he wasn't done. The US Supreme Court hadn't heard his argument and he filed another appeal there, again stressing that the FBI had set him up to squeeze him to assist in recovering the Gardner paintings.

But within six months of the appeals court decision, Turner received word that the US Supreme Court had refused to consider his case. They denied his appeal without giving any opinion as to why.

The past had finally come back to haunt the man the *Boston Globe* had once tagged "the Teflon gangster of the South Shore" of Boston.

For someone who had been arguing for nearly a decade that he had been wrongfully set up by the FBI, the Supreme Court's opinion must have been devastating to Turner. What is certain is that two years later, in March 2010, he wrote to Robert Gentile, a man he had met casually only once or twice before, and asked him to contact an old female friend of Turner's, who in turn asked him to meet with two ex-convicts, a request that Gentile rejected. Turner's Boston lawyer, Robert M. Goldstein, declined comment on the letter.

Goldstein said at some later point he called Gentile's lawyer, A. Ryan McGuigan, in Hartford because Goldstein had heard that Gentile was waiting to decide on whether to cooperate with the authorities depending on what Turner might feel about the decision. Goldstein said he told McGuigan that Gentile needed to decide on his own whether to cooperate, that he did not want to jeopardize Turner being hit with an obstruction of justice charge by the authorities.

Turner refused to discuss why he had written to Gentile but vehemently denied he had done so at the behest of federal officials. As he told me in an e-mail from federal prison in 2013, "First and foremost I have not, nor ever will, cooperate with authorities." But two years later the *Boston Globe* reported that Turner's sentence for his involvement in the armored car robbery scheme had been quietly cut by seven years, now placing his expected release at 2025. Turner and federal prosecutors declined to comment on the sentence reduction, but a spokesman for the US Bureau of Prisons said such actions are customarily taken when a prisoner has provided substantial assistance to federal investigators.

PART IV
A NEW THEORY

CHAPTER NINE

RETHINKING
THE FBI CASE

FOR ALL ITS EXISTING NOTORIETY, the Gardner Museum heist is close to attaining still another superlative: the longest unsolved art theft on the FBI's Most Wanted List.

Of the FBI's list of "top ten art crimes," only the 1969 theft of a Caravaggio from an Italian chapel is older than the Gardner heist. And the loss of the Caravaggio in that case, estimated at $20 million, pales next to the $300 million–$500 million value placed on what was stolen from the Gardner Museum that cold March day in 1990. If the Caravaggio ever comes back, the Gardner heist will be number one in every sense.

Although hopes for a recovery ran high in 2013, after the announcement by the head of the FBI's Boston office that agents knew who had pulled off the theft, the statement, which was in fact made to try to gain the public's help, has led to no breakthrough. Instead, the likelihood of returning the paintings to their still-empty places within the museum seems as remote today as it did in 2010, when the lead FBI agent on the case told me that "in the last twenty years, and the last eight that I've had the case, there hasn't been a concrete sighting, or real proof of life."

Of course, it hasn't been for lack of trying. The FBI has committed tremendous manpower and forensic resources to the case. Even more, it has tried to be creative in coming up with outside-the-box approaches to appeal to those who may know the whereabouts of the artwork, while making clear repeatedly that the statute of limitations on the actual theft ran out in 1995, so the two thieves and anyone who might have participated in the heist cannot be prosecuted.

To those who possess the stolen artwork, federal prosecutors have been equally reassuring: If the pieces are brought back, they have said over and over again, those holding them will not be prosecuted for the outstanding crime of possession of stolen property. And if the pieces are in similar condition to when they were stolen, the holders would be eligible to claim the museum trustees' $5 million reward.

"Short of giving them a ride to the museum, I'm not sure what else we could offer them," former US attorney Donald Stern, who oversaw the investigation for eight years, told me. "This is a no-brainer. It baffles me why they weren't returned long ago."

As for the investigators who have worked the case over the years, two scenarios have been offered as to why the underworld thugs suspected of involvement in the theft and subsequently hiding the art have remained mum, with one being far worse than the other.

In the first, the artwork was hidden—buried even—and the few people who knew where it was stashed have since died. That possibility is considered credible among the street investigators, who realize that knowledge of a theft is tightly held information within the Boston underworld.

Among the Rossetti gang, whose fifteen or so members are believed to have engaged in dozens of robberies, large and small, in the two decades between the early 1970s and mid-1990s, only those who engaged in the actual heist—and its boss, Ralph Rossetti, or his nephew Stephen—might know who did it.

"We were all responsible for coming up with our individual scores," Louis Royce, the Gardner aficionado and member of the Rossetti gang, told me. "Everything had to be cleared by Ralph, or Stevie if Ralph wasn't around. But I didn't want the others knowing what I was up to. It only increased the chances of someone squealing on me if they got caught in something they were doing."

And considering their dangerous line of work, the thieves could have met an untimely death, leaving the artwork in its mysterious hiding place, with perhaps no one left alive with knowledge of the whereabouts.

There's also the distinct possibility that the thieves, in a panic when they learned that their heist had triggered a massive FBI investigation, with forty-five agents assigned to the case at its height, decided that the best thing to do was to get rid of the evidence, destroying the artwork in their desperation.

Two men who traded often in stolen goods have taken very different positions on that possibility.

"It all depends on the circumstances they were in," said William Youngworth. "You're not dealing with stable people who are making decisions in a rational way."

According to Youngworth, the bigger the score, the bigger the scare. And of course, the Gardner was the biggest score of them all.

But Louis Royce, considered by the FBI to be one of Boston's most able thieves, said he and his criminal cohorts never destroyed anything they had stolen, or even threw it away, unless it was a weapon that could tie them to a murder.

"We don't throw anything out, not even the cork of a wine bottle," said Royce, who says he was responsible for dozens of break-ins of homes, jewelry stores, and banks during his criminal career, and who ran a secondhand shop that specialized in stolen goods. "You never know what's going to be valuable tomorrow."

As for the FBI, it places little if any credence in the theory that the artwork was destroyed. Its belief is that the pieces were hidden and, regardless of why, those who are holding them refuse to turn them in.

THE BOSTON MARATHON BOMBING and manhunt, coming so closely on the heels of the FBI's press conference in March 2013, with the promising leads it offered and its appeals to the public for help, effectively stalled the Gardner investigation. Shortly after the bombing, Richard DesLauriers left the FBI and took a job in private industry, leaving sole responsibility for the Gardner case to special agent Geoff Kelly and Gardner security chief Anthony Amore.

DesLauriers stopped responding to inquiries I made about his statements, but Kelly, in a one-on-one interview, added a few specifics to DesLauriers' account: The plot had been hatched in the Dorchester auto body shop where Carmello Merlino, David Turner, and Robert Guarente congregated. And after the theft, Guarente had passed the artwork on to Robert Gentile, the Manchester, Connecticut, hood whose house and surrounding yard investigators had vigorously searched in May 2012.

These names were familiar to me, from the work I and others had done at the *Boston Globe*, but further reporting I had done on their roles gave me pause as to how convincing their involvement in the case might be. Consider some of the evidence we've already seen:

David Turner knew how vulnerable the museum was to a theft through his association with the Rossetti crime gang of East Boston and their man Louis Royce. But the belief that Turner was one of the two thieves seems wishful thinking in light of the credit card receipts I found, showing him in Florida in the days before and after the theft. Perhaps he arranged the theft but did not participate—but then who were his operatives? And how and why would he have coordinated with them while away when the theft could just as well have happened some other day, when he was in town? In any case, Turner's resemblance to the police sketches created at the time of the theft was one of the most compelling pieces of evidence against him. If he was in Florida when the heist happened, this point is irrelevant. Also, Turner was unable to put his hands on the stolen artwork in 1992 when he sought to negotiate with the authorities to gain the release of his crime boss, Carmello Merlino, and closest friend, Charles Pappas, who had been jailed for cocaine trafficking.

Then, nearly a decade later, when authorities pressed Turner to come up with the stolen artwork after he was arrested along with Stevie Rossetti for participating in the scheme to hold up an armored car headquarters, he swore he knew nothing about the whereabouts of the paintings.

Turner is now serving a thirty-year prison sentence. Despite speculation that he might be writing a book about his involvement, he has been behind bars for over fifteen years without any such documents surfacing.

Bobby Guarente is the swingman in the FBI's account. Elene Guarente, his widow, testified to a federal grand jury in 2010, according to one source, that she saw her husband pass several paintings to his cohort Robert Gentile sometime before Guarente died in 2004. Yet in the several telephone interviews

I have had with her she has insisted that she saw her husband pass only one painting to Gentile, and that one did not appear to be any of those stolen from the Gardner Museum. She said she did not recall telling the grand jury that her husband had given more than one painting to Gentile.

With her approval, federal authorities conducted a thorough search of the farmhouse in Madison where her husband lived while in Maine. They found nothing.

And then there's the time she and an old friend of Guarente's approached a lawyer in Boston in 2005 with paint chips that Guarente's daughter, Jeanine, provided, saying they came from the missing Gardner masterpiece *Storm on the Sea of Galilee*. The tests were negative. As a result, the Guarente connection rests on the accounts that were secondhand or could not be corroborated with physical evidence.

As for Robert Gentile, he had every reason to assist the FBI when they approached him in 2010. Although he denied any knowledge of the location of the stolen artwork, his mobster ears perked up when he heard about the $5 million reward. In fact, he went so far as to sign a contract with his lawyer's firm to share a healthy chunk of the reward money if something did develop.

Gentile's life had been spent in search of a big payday, and if the FBI believed his old friend Bobby Guarente had some inside knowledge of the theft and disposal of the artwork, then he was willing to play along with them. But when agents pushed for him to assist David Turner, who attempted to connect with Gentile from federal prison, he hesitated out of concern that it might place him in danger.

Gentile's problems really began, though, when he broke off those discussions completely after agents suggested he introduce an undercover G-man to Turner's underworld cohorts in the hope that the agent might locate a clear path to the artwork. Frustrated, the FBI dispatched an undercover informant to the used car lot where Gentile was working to buy prescription drugs from him. After spurning the overtures at first, Gentile relented. He was soon indicted on—and pleaded guilty to—related charges.

At sentencing a federal prosecutor suggested openly that Gentile had information on the stolen Gardner paintings that he was not sharing with investigators and asked for a stiff sentence of nearly five years in prison in an effort to entice him into talking. But US district judge Robert N. Chatigny rejected the recommendation, ordering Gentile to serve just another year beyond his time already served.

Gentile stayed mum and since being released from federal prison in early 2014 hasn't assisted the authorities or the museum in its quest to regain its stolen paintings. He's bitter over his treatment by the federal investigators after he declined to cooperate with them.

"They ruined my life," Gentile told me, contending that federal efforts to nab him as a drug dealer would never have happened if he had continued to cooperate on the Gardner case. "All because Elene Guarente told them something that they knew wasn't true."

Even two retired FBI agents involved in the investigation dismissed major segments of the sketchy account DesLauriers and Kelly have made public about the Gardner case. Robert Wittman, who worked undercover investigating art thefts for most of his twenty years as an FBI agent, cast doubt on the certainty of the information that the Gardner paintings had been offered for sale to Philadelphia mobsters in 2002.

Wittman said the FBI art theft task force that he worked for during those years was assigned to the FBI's Philadelphia office and his own desk was located "within feet" of the agency's organized crime unit.

"I find it inconceivable that that unit would have picked up word of such a conversation and they're not telling us in our unit about it," Wittman told me.

In light of all this, I had a host of questions I wanted to ask DesLauriers. Unfortunately, he demurred, saying that having retired from the Bureau, he did not want to say anything without FBI approval that might imperil the ongoing investigation.

The FBI, for its part, declined all my requests for interviews.

But another agent, who had worked on the investigation into the criminal activities that Merlino operated out of his Dorchester garage, found it difficult to imagine that members of the same crew had any real connection to the Gardner case. The now-retired agent, who asked not to be identified, said that while the informant picked up much talk by Merlino and others about the possible whereabouts of the Gardner paintings, "it was all bluster."

"If these men at any time knew where those paintings were, they would have turned them over in a heartbeat because of the $5 million reward," the agent said.

As for DesLauriers' claims at the 2013 press conference?

"I imagine that it was a convenient story to tell to get more people to pay attention," the retired agent said.

This made perfect sense as I struggled to understand why the FBI had provided such scant—and, as it turned out, debatable—details of its investigation. Regardless of what Des-Lauriers and Kelly had said about what the FBI investigation had uncovered, in the end it didn't matter how strong their case was regarding the involvement of Merlino, Turner, Guarente, or Gentile. Merlino and Guarente were dead, and Turner and Gentile had both gone to jail after rejecting offers from the FBI to make deals for what they knew about the paintings.

The ultimate goal of the investigation now was not to prosecute anyone for the theft or for hiding the artwork. Accurate information—hard evidence—was needed for arrests and criminal court cases, but with the statute of limitations having run out, no such prosecutions are part of the plan.

The purpose of the 2013 press conference and DesLauriers' sensational, if unspecific, assertions were to draw maximum public attention to the special website the FBI had established to show what the thirteen stolen pieces looked like. Most people might know immediately what Rembrandt's *Storm on the Sea of Galilee* or Vermeer's *The Concert* looked like if they happened upon them in the attic or the trunk of a long-lost relative. But what about the eleven less-recognizable pieces, such as Manet's portrait or the five Degas sketches?

Getting an accurate account of what had happened in the pre-dawn hours of March 18, 1990, what had motivated the largest art theft in world history, and where the stolen pieces had been stashed was the priority of reporters like me. The ultimate, if not only, aim of the FBI's Boston office, however, was to return those paintings to the museum's gallery walls. By using what the FBI had learned—or perhaps, even more, what it appeared to have learned—from its success in capturing Whitey Bulger, the FBI felt they could find this out by piquing public interest.

As DesLauriers stated in closing his remarks at his March 2013 press conference: "To close the book on this theft we need to recover the art and return it to its rightful owner. We are calling upon the American public to assist us in this investigation, as they have so many times before."

And then, not long after the Boston Marathon bombing took everyone's attention away from the Gardner press conference, just as it seemed that the secrets of the Gardner case would die in the murky Boston underworld, a call from a rival gang would call into question all of the FBI's assumptions.

CHAPTER TEN

A TALE OF
TWO GANGS

THE BOSTON MOB in the 1980s was in complete chaos.
After Raymond Patriarca, an Italian mobster who had
ruled the New England mob with an iron fist for more than
thirty years, died in 1984, leaving control with his son, there
was a scramble for primacy among the gangland thugs.

Raymond Junior was neither as smart nor as brutal as his
father. After all, who could have been as tough as the man who
had ordered a man under his control to kill his own son because a deal-gone-wrong had cost Patriarca money? Struggling
to live up to his dad's *Godfather*-like reputation, the younger
Patriarca had a tentative grip on things, at best.

A second shock hit the Boston underworld when Gennaro
Angiulo, who with his brothers ran the city's criminal organization as Patriarca's underboss, was indicted and jailed.

For several years, with no single individual emerging
with the necessary power and prestige to lead the underworld,

several smaller rings that had operated under Patriarca and Angiulo's authority jockeyed for control. One such group, out of Boston's North End, included the mob soldiers Vincent A. Ferrara, Joseph A. "J. R." Russo, and Angelo "Sonny" Mercurio.

And of course, there was South Boston mobster James "Whitey" Bulger, who had the force and toughness to carve out his own place in Boston's mob scene. Bulger operated independently of the Angiulos, yet had been as murderous as any gang leader in America. Two obstacles stood in Bulger's way, however. He wasn't Italian and, in 1988, it was revealed in a series by the *Boston Globe* that he had enjoyed a "special relationship" with the FBI as a key underworld informant.

On the cusp of that revelation, when all-out war seemed inevitable, one of Bulger's allies, Frank "Cadillac" Salemme, was released from jail. Salemme faced neither of Bulger's obstacles in seeking leadership of the Boston mob, and he immediately began to consolidate his control.

One of Salemme's first moves was to persuade Raymond Patriarca Jr. that, as titular head of the New England mob, he had the clout to name Salemme as his Boston underboss. Although they believed—mistakenly as it turned out—that Patriarca would not give Salemme the blessing he was seeking, Vinnie Ferrara and J. R. Russo waited to see which way Patriarca Jr. would go. They didn't have to wait too long.

In June 1989, Salemme was lured to a meeting outside a pancake restaurant in Saugus by Sonny Mercurio, a Patriarca gang member who later turned mob informant, and was ambushed.

Salemme was badly wounded—shot in the chest and leg—but he survived. Those responsible for the ambush were never prosecuted.

Then Patriarca Jr., in a half-baked effort to bring peace among the warring factions, approved a ceremony in which foot soldiers of both gangs would be inducted into the mafia. It was intended to be the most formal of ceremonies, with vows

Frank Salemme led a criminal gang that sought to take over Boston's underworld after Gennaro Angiulo; his brothers were indicted and removed from the scene in the mid-1980s. Salemme is shown here (left, in white) with members of his inner circle, including Richard Devlin (second from right). Courtesy *Boston Globe*

of loyalty underscored with the sharing of blood from pricked fingers, but unfortunately for Patriarca, several members of the group crowded into the basement of a Medford residence owned by the relative of a mob underling were FBI informants.

To top it off, the whole ceremony was bugged by the Boston office of the FBI.

Patriarca began the meeting by saying that, to bring peace between the two groups—Salemme's and the one Russo, Ferrara, and Robert Carrozza controlled—he had agreed to make his stepbrother J. R. Russo his consigliere in Boston. Both sides would agree to abide by Russo's decisions, he told those attending. Then, with the FBI picking up the entire session through an extraordinary "roving bug" from outside the house, the ceremony began.

Each would-be mobster took the same oath in Italian, following the lead of Biagio DiGiacomo, the balding, pudgy-faced captain of the Patriarca family.

"I want to enter into this organization to protect my family and to protect all of my friends. I swear to not divulge this secret and to obey with love and *omerta*."

Each inductee's trigger finger was then pricked, drawing blood for use in the ceremony. Eventually a holy card, with the image of the patron saint of the Patriarca family, was burned in the hands of each inductee.

"As burns this saint, so will burn my soul," DiGiacomo read. "I want to enter alive into this organization and I will have to get out dead."

Then, in an ominous, almost monotone voice, DiGiacomo stressed the importance of the secret oath taken by the inductees.

"It's no hope, no Jesus, no Madonna," DiGiacomo warned. "Nobody can help us if we ever give up this secret to anybody. Any kinds of friends of mine, let's say. This thing that cannot be exposed."

When it was discovered that the induction ceremony had been compromised by the FBI—compounding the doubts the other families already had about Patriarca Jr.—the son's hopes of controlling the New England mob evaporated. His only recourse was to "go to the mattresses": an all-out war between the two Boston crime rings. The soldiers controlled by Salemme took on those controlled by Ferrara, Carrozza, and Russo, a gang known as the "renegade group" because they owed their allegiance more to the Angiulos in Boston than the Patriarcas out of Providence.

The hostility between the two gangs was so intense that it touched off more than a dozen murders and assassination attempts, and all efforts to bring peace following the attempt to kill Salemme in 1989 failed miserably. And when the innocent son of one soldier in the renegade group was killed fixing a flat tire, the situation only intensified.

"This was a very dangerous time," said one member of East Boston's Rossetti family, which was loyal to Salemme.

"People were looking over their shoulder all the time. It wasn't good for business, and it wasn't good for anyone's health."

Both sides drew up assassination lists of who was most vulnerable and in what order they should be hit, according to a 1994 indictment that resulted in the arrest of more than two dozen members of both gangs and put a halt to the outright warfare.

"I left right then," the Rossetti family member told me, after hearing his name was on a list prepared by the Russo/Ferrara gang and two strangers showed up at his sister's house asking for him. "I went as far north as I could in New England, changed my name and never came back."

IN THE EARLY DAYS of the war between the Salemme and Ferrara/Carrozza/Russo factions, as the two gangs tried to kill each other in shocking numbers to exert control over Boston's underworld, a few members in each camp shared a common secret: that the Gardner Museum was vulnerable to a theft.

The Rossetti gang, whose members were loyal to Salemme, knew by way of Louis Royce, the gay mobster who had slept inside the museum as a child.

After the theft—but before Frank Salemme disappeared into the witness protection program—I asked a member of his family if Salemme might be able to shed some light on the theft and the whereabouts of the paintings. A few days later I got word back from Salemme.

"He says he doesn't know anything himself but would have to talk to Stevie Rossetti to know for sure," I was told. At the time Rossetti was serving more than forty years in prison for bringing multiple weapons and bombs to the armored car heist he'd planned with David Turner and others in 1999.

And at least one member of the Ferrara/Carrozza/Russo gang knew because he had hung out with the legendary art thief Myles Connor and, with Connor, had cased the Gardner Museum back in the 1980s.

Although law enforcement and even the Gardner Museum had investigated countless leads over the years, the secret of who had actually pulled off the Gardner heist lay within these two gangs. At war since the mid-1980s, the gangs still shared connections. And those connections might just unlock the mystery of the March 1990 theft at the Gardner Museum.

CHAPTER ELEVEN

THE MISSING MOTIVE

ON A SATURDAY EVENING IN MAY 2014, my home phone rang.
I didn't recognize the number that showed up on my
caller ID, so by habit I reverted back to my years as a *Boston
Globe* reporter, giving my full name when I picked up. About a
month before, I had written a letter to Vincent Ferrara, the former Boston gang leader, after hearing that he had told a lawyer
I knew that he was interested in helping solve the Gardner
mystery. After introducing himself, the caller, who asked to
remain anonymous and identified as an intermediary to Ferrara, questioned what I knew about the Gardner Museum theft,
and why I was interested in talking to Ferrara, whom he said
he knew. Soon he sought my theory on the case.

"I've been at this a long time," I told the caller. "But really,
I just don't know. I'll tell you one thing, though; the FBI is
damn sure they know."

"Oh yeah?" the caller said.

I told him that as far as I could tell, the FBI was certain the heist had been arranged by David Turner, who had turned the stolen art over to Robert Guarente, who before he died in 2004 had given at least several of the paintings to Robert Gentile.

"Do you believe them?" the caller asked.

"I know there are holes in their story on all counts," I replied. "But I don't see any reason for the feds to be lying about what they've come up with."

"They don't know what they're talking about," the caller said. "David Turner didn't have anything to do with this. If he did, he wouldn't be spending the best years of his life behind bars.

"Bobby Donati robbed the Gardner Museum," the caller said flatly.

"Why would Donati pull off a heist like that in 1990?" I asked the caller.

"To get Vinnie Ferrara out of jail," he responded.

BY THE LATE 1980S, Vincent Ferrara had ascended to the top level of a Boston-area group that was trying to assert control of the New England underworld. Although he'd been inducted into the Patriarca family and was regarded as a cunning strategist and fierce enforcer of the mob's rules, Ferrara was a different sort from his brothers in his own gang, not to mention the gang headed by Frank Salemme that he was battling for control.

Ferrara hadn't grown up around the mob, like most of his consorts. In fact, once upon a time Ferrara had been headed for a career in finance. Then he started hanging around with the toughs in Boston's North End. After he was convicted for illegal possession of a firearm in the mid-1970s, his chances of convincing legitimate people to trust him with their money evaporated and he turned to offering protection to bookies, loan sharks, and their brethren.

Even more unusual in his line of work, Ferrara was different in how he maintained his personal life. He was obsessed with healthy living. He'd never smoked and had avoided eating red meat since the late 1970s. He worked out religiously, was a voracious reader, and was a good enough high school student to have been accepted at Boston College, where he'd graduated with a degree in finance. But more akin to his fellow mobsters, he maintained strict adherence to the mafia code that all key decisions and conflicts were to be handled by the heads of the families, and that its members were strictly forbidden from engaging in drug trafficking.

According to those who knew him, Ferrara told of conversations he had had with mob boss Jerry Angiulo on how he should conduct himself if he expected to succeed in business or in the mob. "Don't do business with anyone unless you think he's as strong and smart as you are," Angiulo had told him, according to one Ferrara associate. Ferrara heeded that advice, believing the old man meant that while anyone can be your partner when times are good, when things get screwed up, you want to be sure you've got someone beside you who isn't going to panic and who is going to back you up no matter what you decide to do.

The war between the two gangs had been going on since US prosecutors had indicted the Angiulo brothers on multiple counts of racketeering in 1985.

Jerry Angiulo and his brothers had maintained an iron grip over Boston's bookmaking, loan-sharking, and other criminal activity since Raymond Patriarca had anointed him as underboss of most of New England's organized crime activity in the early 1970s. Secret tape recordings of the North End office Angiulo used to run his criminal enterprise proved to be his undoing. In conversations intercepted by the FBI, Angiulo bragged to Ilario Zannino, his consigliere, of his organization's powerful reach and his belief that he and his associates couldn't be indicted for racketeering, believing the offense applied only to the illegal takeover of legitimate businesses and not of illegitimate ones.

"Our argument is we're illegitimate business," Angiulo told Zannino, describing the legal defense he would raise to any indictment. "We're shylocks," Zannino agreed.

"We're shylocks," Angiulo echoed. "We're fuckin' bookmakers."

"Bookmakers," parroted Zannino.

"We're selling marijuana," Angiulo picked up.

"We're not infiltrating," Zannino added.

"We're illegal here, illegal there," Angiulo continued. "Arsonists. We're every fuckin' thing."

"Pimps, prostitutes," Zannino picked up.

"The law doesn't cover us," Angiulo stated boldly. "Is that right?"

"That's the argument," Zannino replied.

Angiulo turned out to be wrong and the feds convicted him of an avalanche of criminal charges. In February 1986 he was sentenced to forty-five years in prison. Angiulo died in 2009 following his release from federal prison. The battle between Salemme and Ferrara to succeed Angiulo as Boston's crime underboss began almost immediately after his conviction. Raymond Patriarca had died two years before, so there was no ultimate authority to choose a successor. The decision would be made by the power of the gun.

It was under these circumstances that Frank Salemme was nearly killed, and soon thereafter, Raymond Patriarca Jr. held the ill-fated cease-fire talks that the FBI secretly recorded. Rather than re-securing Patriarca's hold on the Boston underworld, the events of that day essentially guaranteed his fall from power.

For his part, Ferrara was undone by a different set of tapes. In early 1987, he summoned two aging bookies, Moe Weinstein and Harry "Doc" Sagansky, to Vanessa's, a mob-friendly restaurant in downtown Boston. There he informed them that the old ways of doing things under the Angiulos were changing. No longer would they be allowed to operate their booking operations rent-free.

Both would need to pay $1,500 each month in tribute to Ferrara, and each would need to come up with a $500,000 pay-off just to stay in business.

"I'm not making that kind of money," Doc Sagansky, who had operated a bookmaking business in Boston for fifty years, told Ferrara. His traditional moneymaker, the daily three- and four-digit numbers games, had been made obsolete by the state-run Massachusetts Lottery.

"What I'm driving at," Sagansky told Ferrara plainly, "is that the business has been destroyed. You pick up the paper and look at the payoffs on the four numbers and three numbers, and the four numbers is almost 100 percent more if you play with the lottery. . . . I don't know if you ever look at it. We look at it because . . ."

Ferrara finished the sentence for him. "It's your business."

As it turned out Sonny Mercurio, Ferrara's close friend and the best man at his second wedding, had turned FBI informant and had arranged for the feds to secretly tape Ferrara's meeting with Sagansky and Weinstein. The tapes would ultimately be the underpinning of the racketeering indictment against Ferrara and eight others.

But the tapes weren't Ferrara's only problem. He was also indicted for ordering the murder of Vincent "Jimmy" Limoli, whom federal prosecutors tried to show Ferrara wanted killed because he had persisted in selling drugs in the North End. Ferrara's lawyers claimed that the prosecution's lead witness on the murder charge was lying about Ferrara's involvement but it would take twenty years and the unearthing of long-buried government files for that defense to be upheld.

In the early 1990s, however, Ferrara, who was forty at the time, was convinced that he faced a life sentence if he went to trial on the murder charge and was convicted. Believing his only recourse was a plea deal, he pleaded guilty to second-degree murder and in 1992 he was sentenced to twenty-two years in jail.

Bobby Donati was one of the first people to visit him in jail. The two had been close for nearly a decade, as Ferrara was growing in power in the Boston underworld, and when Ferrara needed someone he could trust to be his driver, he picked Donati.

Donati was the perfect wheelman for Ferrara. The two had spent hours at a time together in Donati's red Mercedes two-seater through much of the 1980s, and Donati, a perennial jokester, kept the conversation light. That is, except when he was broke, which was most of the time, and he was looking for advice from Ferrara on whom he could tap for a quick loan or to find an easy score. Donati had an appreciation for the finer things in life, including oriental rugs and antiques, and spent many weekends visiting museums, galleries, and second-hand shops with his son.

But that day in the federal lockup in Hartford, where Ferrara was first taken after his arrest, Donati was deadly serious, according to a source who knew both men.

"I can't let you stay here," Donati told Ferrara, keeping his words clipped and vague as both men knew that conversations between prisoners and their visitors were likely tapped, according to the source. "I'm going to get you out of here."

"What are you talking about?" Ferrara asked Donati. "Don't you do anything. No matter what you do, it's not going to get me out of here."

"They will for these; you'll see," Donati said.

Vincent Ferrara (left) and Robert Donati (right) enjoy a meal with an unidentified third man sometime before Ferrara was arrested for racketeering in November 1989—three months before the Gardner Museum was robbed. Donati allegedly told Ferrara he arranged the heist to assist in bartering for Ferrara's release.

"Bobby, don't do this," Ferrara implored, according to the source. "Whatever it is you've got planned, do not do it. You're just going to get yourself in trouble. Besides, they're not letting me out of here no matter what you're offering."

But three months later, Ferrara read the news that two men dressed as police officers had stolen thirteen pieces of art, including several masterpieces, from Boston's Gardner Museum, and he knew immediately who was behind it.

Ferrara had been moved back to Massachusetts and was incarcerated in the Plymouth House of Correction when Donati came to see him. "Was that you?" he asked Donati, the source recounted.

"I told you I was going to do it. Now I got to find a way to begin negotiating to get you out," Donati responded.

"You're insane," Ferrara responded, remembering that the headlines had said the Gardner heist might be the largest art theft ever and that the FBI had more than forty agents scouring

Boston's neighborhoods for clues. "They're not going to do any deal where they have to let me out. They want me locked up forever, now more than ever," the source said, quoting Ferrara.

The Justice Department was indeed intent on eliminating Boston's mob. US attorney general Richard Thornburgh and FBI director William Sessions had even traveled to Boston in a government jet to announce the indictments, saying they represented the most sweeping attack on a single organized crime family.

"The case is important in that it represents a stake in the heart of a major organized crime family from the boss on down," Thornburgh said at a press conference. "It establishes beyond doubt the existence of a secret clandestine operation that takes itself very seriously in terms of the illegal operations it carries out." Although the press conference took place eight days after the Gardner theft, nothing was said about the status of the investigation.

But the heist was certainly on Ferrara's mind when Donati sat across from him at the Plymouth jail. "Bobby, you're going to bring more heat on yourself than ever before," Ferrara said, actually sounding genuinely concerned for his fellow mobster. "For your own good, I'm telling you to get out of town. Go to Florida. Anywhere. But get out of town."

"Don't worry about me," Donati said, seemingly unfazed. "I've buried the stuff. Once this blows over, I'll find the right person to negotiate with."

Donati never got that far. He was brutally murdered in September 1991, sixteen months after the theft. The FBI had him under continuous surveillance at the time. It is possible the feds believed he was a vulnerable target in Boston's ongoing gang war—or they may have been looking at him as a suspect in the Gardner case.

There has long been evidence linking Donati to the Gardner heist. His name had surfaced in connection with the museum in 1997 because of his association with legendary Boston art thief Myles Connor. But this account provided by the source, of Donati visiting Ferrara to tell him of his plans to get him out of prison, has never been disclosed before.

The story is a reminder of the importance of one of the most elemental aspects of detective work. From the time Louis Royce first began casing it in 1981, the Gardner Museum's poor security was an opportunity staring every Boston criminal in the face. Turner and Guarente may have fit the profile. And Rossetti may have had the means. But in the person of his recently arrested boss, Bobby Donati had something no one else had: a motive.

———

VINNIE FERRARA is not the only person who believes Bobby Donati was one of the two men who carried out the greatest art theft in world history. Myles Connor, the son of a police chief who turned into a legendary art thief in New England, says he was told the same thing—by Donati's alleged partner in the crime, a similar ne'er-do-well named David Houghton.

Houghton had long been friends with Connor, sharing Connor's love of rock music and often accompanying Connor to gigs his band would get in and around Boston. Like Donati with Ferrara, Houghton had taken it personally when Connor was arrested on a drug deal gone wrong in 1989 and was sentenced to ten years in federal prison. Around the same time in mid-1990 that Donati was visiting Ferrara at the Plymouth House of Correction to tell him of the Gardner robbery, Houghton was flying to Lompoc federal prison in southern California to visit Connor.

"You think I was going to let you rot to death here?" Houghton asked Connor. "Me and Bobby Donati did that score, and we're going to use the paintings to get you out," Connor recalled Houghton telling him.

To this day, Connor believes Donati was involved in the Gardner theft, saying they often discussed how vulnerable the museum was to being ripped off. Also, he says when they first met in the early 1970s, Donati was already familiar with how useful stealing valuable art was. In his book, *The Art of the Heist*, Connor wrote that Donati had shown him how easy it would be to break into the Woolworth Estate in Monmouth, Maine. In May 1974 they stole five stunning paintings by Andrew Wyeth and his father, N. C. Wyeth from the estate.

Connor says he stashed the Wyeth paintings with his girlfriend in western Massachusetts, then went looking for someone who was interested in purchasing valuable, albeit stolen, art. After rejecting overtures from several gallery owners, Connor says, he thought he had found the right person, on an introduction through Donati. The two men agreed to meet in the parking lot of a Cape Cod shopping center.

But instead of being interested buyers, the individual was an undercover FBI agent, and Connor was arrested.

Once out on bail, Connor continued his life of crime, robbing a bank and then setting his sights on Boston's Museum of Fine Arts. With the trial for his theft of the Wyeth paintings only months away, Connor figured the only way he could gain leverage against federal prosecutors was to make an even bigger score.

On a sunny April morning in 1975, Connor drove with two friends to the MFA in Boston's Fens neighborhood. With one pal parked outside, Connor and another man made their way into the museum and headed for the second floor. There they pulled a large Rembrandt painting called *Girl with a Fur-Trimmed Cloak* from the wall and ran from the building. A guard gave chase and quickly caught up to the pair. He grabbed the painting but was bludgeoned with the butt end of a rifle and decided to

Robert A. Donati (following an arrest in the 1980s)
cased the Gardner Museum for robbery with legendary
Boston art thief Myles Connor Jr., with whom he had
robbed a Maine estate of valuable paintings in the 1970s.
Donati was amazed when he learned that Connor's
lawyer had been able to secure a plea deal with federal
authorities by promising to return stolen artwork.

give up his grip rather than risk his life for the painting. Connor stashed it underneath the bed of his best friend's mother.

Several months later, with the federal trial for his role in the theft of the Wyeth paintings about to take place, Connor reached out to the Massachusetts state police and the assistant US attorney prosecuting the federal case through his lawyer, Martin Leppo. If the authorities entertain a plea deal, Leppo told them, Connor would facilitate the return of the Rembrandt.

"Negotiating for stolen art is a controversial subject," Connor wrote in his autobiography. "Certainly none of them [in law enforcement] wanted to be seen making a deal with a convicted cop shooter and known art thief."

But that's exactly what Connor and Leppo were able to arrange. In exchange for the return of the Rembrandt, prosecutors dropped the charges of bail jumping against Connor after he had failed to show up for one hearing. And the US attorney's office agreed to recommend that the four-year sentence against Connor in the Wyeth thefts run concurrently with the sentence imposed for the MFA robbery.

Donati clearly marveled at Connor's ability to swap the return of a stolen masterpiece for leniency within the federal and state court systems. At the same time Connor was completing his sweetheart deal with the US attorney's office in Boston, Donati was seeking something similar from a federal judge. He wrote to US district court judge W. Arthur Garrity Jr., asking for reduction in a ten-year sentence Garrity had imposed on him following Donati's guilty plea on stolen securities charges. Donati had been serving a state prison sentence, during which he'd participated in a work release program. If Garrity checked with state correction officials, Donati argued, he would find that Donati had become a model prisoner while serving in that program, and deserved a reduction in the federal prison term he was now facing.

"I am not asking that I be released overnight, but only that I be afforded some relief so I can go back into work release and continue my upward strides so that I need never come back into these places again," Donati wrote.

But unlike Connor, Donati had nothing to trade for his freedom, certainly no Rembrandt. Garrity denied Donati's motion.

Despite their disparate treatment by the court system, Connor and Donati remained friends both inside and outside prison in the ensuing years. After discussing how easy it would be to rob the Gardner, the two men even visited the museum on several occasions, with Donati paying particular attention to the security desk and the guard manning it, Connor said.

What's more, Donati was dropping suspicious hints to others at the key time. Just before the robbery took place, Donati walked into a Revere, Massachusetts, social club called The Shack, run by his close friend, Donny "The Hat" Roquefort. Donati carried a large paper bag under his arm and Roquefort insisted that Donati show him what was inside. When Donati resisted, the larger and tougher Roquefort approached him and grabbed the bag, and ripped it open. Two police uniforms fell out of it.

"What the hell, have you joined the other side?" Roquefort shouted at Donati playfully, and grabbed the taser stun gun he usually kept beneath The Shack's front counter. He pressed the taser playfully into Donati's side and pulled the trigger—it must have been the first time Roquefort had used the taser, as the blast of the gun did quite a number on Donati, burning right through his coat, shirt, and into his skin.

Donati never explained what he was doing with the uniforms, but at least one person there that day remembered the odd encounter with the taser gun. And this source said there was one other person with Donati at the Shack that day: Bobby Guarente.

Indeed, according to members of both men's families, Guarente and Donati had long been close. Donati's close relationship with Guarente provides the most tantalizing clue to his possible connection to the Gardner theft. In the FBI's view, Guarente played a central role in the heist. He received the paintings, they believe, from small-time hoods such as Carmello Merlino and David Turner at Merlino's Dorchester auto body shop. Then, they believe, Guarente held onto the paintings at his home in Maine until the early 2000s, when, after learning he had cancer, he turned the paintings over to Robert Gentile, the low-level hood based in Manchester, Connecticut. In the late 1990s, when Guarente ran a cocaine distribution ring out of a home in suburban Boston, Gentile worked for him as a cook, poker dealer, and part-time security man.

Elene Guarente, Guarente's widow, remembers Donati fondly. "My Bobby was close to Bobby Donati. They knew each other as teenagers. Bobby even brought his son on a fishing trip up to our place in Maine."

When Donati disappeared in September 1991, Guarente was one of the first individuals that members of Donati's family called to see where he might be.

According to sources who knew him, Donati wasn't prepared for the level of police attention devoted to the Gardner theft. It's easy to envision the scenario: afraid for his safety, he buries the paintings for a time, until the furor died down. Then, sometime in 1990 or 1991, he passes one or several of the works to someone he trusts: Bobby Guarente.

Earle Berghman, the close friend of Guarente's in Maine, is convinced the friendship between Guarente and Donati included dealings on the Gardner paintings. "Bobby Donati did that job," he said of the Gardner theft. "Then he gave some of them [paintings] to Guarente when he became concerned about his own safety. Bobby Donati knew he was a marked man. Why else would he give over the thing he valued most—those paintings—to Bobby Guarente? Then, before Guarente died, he passed them on to Gentile in Connecticut."

The brutality of Donati's death is particularly troubling for his family members, because he was under FBI surveillance in the weeks before it. He was attacked as he walked onto the front porch of his modest home on Mountain Avenue in Revere, a working-class Boston suburb. His body was found bludgeoned and stabbed twenty-one times, stuffed in the trunk of his white Cadillac, about a half mile from his home. Donati had become withdrawn and anxious and seldom ventured out of his house before his death. He'd told one associate about a month before he was killed that he'd noticed two suspicious men in black running suits hanging around his house and figured they were plotting to kill him.

Why the FBI had Donati under surveillance at this time, or whether agents suspected he had been marked for assassination, is not stated in his FBI file. However, the files note that Donati owed a large amount of cash to local bookmakers. Others speculated that with Ferrara, his protector, locked up, Donati had been attacked by members of the rival gang headed by "Cadillac Frank" Salemme. No one has ever been charged in Donati's murder.

Lorraine Donati is haunted by her brother's savage killing and has tried without luck to get answers from investigators about the circumstances of his death, and even whether he might have had anything to do with the Gardner case.

"One bullet could have accomplished what they were looking to do," Lorraine Donati says ruefully of her brother's execution. "No one has to be stabbed and beaten like that unless there was some dark secret behind it. I go to bed every night angry or sad that I don't know, and I seem to be the only one who feels that way."

As for Ferrara, the theft of the Gardner artwork made no difference in his years in prison. He bounced between federal prisons throughout the country during the next decade, but after learning that one of his closest associates had been a government informant against him, he decided to appeal his conviction. In going through the evidence against him, his lawyers learned that a key witness against Ferrara had recanted his testimony to the police, that Ferrara had not ordered the killing of his associate. However, that information had never been turned over to Ferrara's lawyers.

In 2005 a federal district court reopened Ferrara's case after long-buried evidence surfaced showing Ferrara had no involvement in the killing of a young gang associate who had been dealing in drugs. US district judge Mark L. Wolf took two actions once he learned of the new evidence: He recommended that the Justice Department investigate the federal prosecutor who'd kept the information buried for sixteen years, and he found that Ferrara had served long enough on his racketeering charges and should be released immediately.

After listening to five hours of recorded telephone conversations Ferrara had made while in prison during the previous year, Wolf was convinced that Ferrara was sincere in his promise to go straight. The phone calls "demonstrate that Ferrara remains deeply dedicated to his family, and is both able to obey rules and determined to do so in the future," Wolf said.

"Having had the opportunity to observe Ferrara closely over many years, this court finds Ferrara's statement to be sincere and meaningful," Wolf said of the former mob leader's pledge to live a law-abiding and peaceful life if he was released from prison.

For an ex-mobster to receive such a ringing personal endorsement from a federal judge appears remarkable in retrospect, but in the decade since his release, Ferrara has made good on his pledge to stay out of trouble and avoid association with any of his past criminal cohorts. He lives a quiet life, sharing a condominium with his son on the outskirts of the North End, keeping in close touch with his four daughters and six grandchildren.

DURING THE WEEK AFTER I got my surprise phone call, I had several conversations with the caller, who had personal knowledge of the talks between Donati and Ferrara. I also sought confirmation from Ferrara himself but, as he'd done to others who had approached him to talk since his release from federal prison in 2005, he declined to be interviewed.

"Why are you telling me this now?" I asked the caller. It was nearly twenty-five years after the theft, and ten years after Ferrara's release from prison, after all. There were several reasons, I was told, to come forward with the story. Not the least of these was the $5 million reward the museum was offering for the paintings' safe return; like everyone else in Boston, Ferrara certainly had an interest in that. And, I was told, he'd pledged to share the reward with Donati's son and other members of the Donati family. Ferrara would also lobby for the release—or at least a reduction in his long prison sentence—of David Turner, his old cohort in Boston's underworld, whom he felt had been set up by the authorities to find out what Turner knew about the Gardner theft.

Also, for someone who values greatly how he is viewed in the city of his upbringing, the caller said, Ferrara believed that facilitating the return of the artwork would go a long way toward improving his reputation.

Having checked my caller's information with several who know both men, including Elene Guarente and members of Bobby Donati's family, I decided to relay what I'd learned to the FBI. Special agent Geoffrey Kelly, the FBI's lead on the Gardner investigation for more than a decade, and Anthony Amore, still the head of security at the Gardner, agreed to see me. I had met both men numerous times in the past, but on each of those occasions it was me asking the questions and taking notes. This time it was different; I was doing the talking and Kelly and Amore took the notes.

For nearly an hour, I told them about my conversations with the caller, and the detailed information he'd provided about conversations between Ferrara and Donati. Specifically, I told them about the places my caller suggested Donati might have buried any stolen artwork, including the house he'd rented on Mountain Avenue in Revere, his mother's home in Everett, and the New Hampshire home his former wife was living in at the time of the theft. I also offered one further opportunity: If the pair had any doubt about what I was telling them, my caller was willing to meet with Amore—though not Kelly—to answer any further questions he might have.

"Everyone knows I've never talked to the feds," the caller had said, when I'd pressed him on why he would not meet with Kelly. "Besides, I don't want people speculating that I'm in some kind of trouble, because I'm not."

I gave Amore the caller's cell phone number, but he never called him. Nor did he—or Kelly—return my subsequent phone calls when I tried to determine what they'd thought of the information I had relayed to them, and what, if anything, they planned to do with it.

Less than a month later, though, Kelly gave a clear indication of what he thought about the information I had passed on to him suggesting that Robert Donati had been instrumental in pulling off the theft from the Gardner Museum. In an exclusive interview with the Fox News local Boston outlet about the Gardner heist, Kelly made no mention of Donati as knowing anything about the Gardner heist. Instead, Kelly stressed that there had been "sightings" of the stolen artwork by individuals the FBI believed were worthwhile sources—clearly contradicting the story I'd told them. Kelly declined to identify the individuals in question, or say where the sightings had taken place.

THAT THE SECRET of the greatest art heist in world history might rest within the dynamics of the Boston gang war has not been lost on Anne Hawley. Although the war between the Salemme and Ferrara/Russo gangs was a tremendous concern for law enforcement for more than a decade between the mid-1980s and mid-1990s, leading to more than a dozen killings and several major trials, the Gardner theft was never raised seriously as a possible motive or even topic of inquiry in any of those cases.

"I just can't understand it," Hawley thought as the years ticked by after the theft. "Here we have this gang war going on, with Whitey Bulger and all that making front-page news, yet no one ever gets questioned about the Gardner case."

Hawley made her own approaches. In the late 1990s, after a federal judge had held hearings into the FBI's secret dealings with Whitey Bulger and other informants, she reached out to *Boston Herald* reporter Ralph Ranalli, who had covered them, and asked if any possible links to the Gardner case had surfaced. No, sorry, he said. When William Bulger, president of the Massachusetts Senate, made one of his frequent visits to the museum, she approached him. Would he be willing to ask his brother, Whitey, what he might know or be able to learn about the stolen artwork? Bulger never answered the question and changed the subject quickly.

Investigators, however, have long been intrigued that Whitey Bulger might have had something to do with the Gardner robbery, or known who was responsible for it. US attorney Michael Sullivan went so far as to ask Stephen Flemmi, Bulger's closest associate, who testified against him at his 2013 trial, if Bulger had any connection to the theft.

Flemmi told him that following the theft, Bulger had directed him to find out who was responsible. In effect, Flemmi told Sullivan, Bulger had told him "no one pulls off a heist like that in my territory without paying me tribute."

Disgraced FBI agent John Connolly, who had handled Bulger as an informant, said that even though he was retired from the Bureau when the theft took place, he was asked by his old colleagues to see what he could find out from Bulger.

"It was the same thing," Connolly said. "He wanted to know so he could get his percentage, but he couldn't find anything out."

The FBI has persistently shown little interest in pursuing Donati as a suspect. Despite Donati's name being raised as being responsible, neither his sister nor his ex-wife had ever been questioned by authorities about his possible role. Nor did authorities ever search the Revere home Donati was renting at the time of his death for any signs of the paintings.

Instead, Kelly insisted that the FBI remained focused on three men who were "persons of interest" at the center of their investigation: Carmello Merlino, owner of the Dorchester auto body repair shop who had died in federal prison in 1998 after being convicted of attempted robbery of an armored car headquarters; Robert Guarente, the gangster who died in 2004 soon after his release from federal prison after serving a six-year sentence for cocaine trafficking; and Robert Gentile, the low-level hood who for years was close to Guarente and who has consistently denied he had any role in the Gardner heist or in stashing the paintings.

Regardless of their ties to the Gardner case, what does link Merlino, Guarente, and Gentile to the case is their affiliation to "Cadillac Frank" Salemme and his gang, who were not only fighting Vincent Ferrara for dominance of Boston's mob underworld. Both gangs also knew how vulnerable the Gardner Museum was to being robbed.

Bobby Donati was the guy in Vincent Ferrara's crew who had always had his eyes on the Gardner, mostly because of his longstanding relationship with Myles Connor, Boston's legendary art thief. Meanwhile, the Salemme gang knew about the woeful security guarding the Gardner's riches from members of the Rossetti family, who had of course learned of it through master thief Louis Royce.

Royce had told two people—Stephen Rossetti, the nephew of gang leader Ralph Rossetti, and Richard Devlin, an enforcer for underboss Salemme—about his days hiding out in the Gardner, of its poor security, and even how to rob the museum.

But although Stevie Rossetti had helped pull off the art heist from the home in Newton with his uncle and Royce in 1981, he'd told another associate who reminded him of Royce's tales of the Gardner's vulnerability while driving by the museum one night, "I'm not interested in art. That's Louis' score." Most tellingly, though, Rossetti continues to serve a forty-plus-year sentence for participation in the armored car heist in 1999, when offering the authorities information on the Gardner investigation would clearly prompt them to reduce his prison term.

As for Richard Devlin, the second gang member Royce told about the museum's vulnerability, he was a brutal enforcer. Devlin had gone to jail for dismembering a Dorchester tough in 1972 and, once released, specialized in robbing armored cars. He was so active that in the mid-1980s the authorities put together a joint federal-state task force to crack down on the surge of armored car robberies he had inspired in New York, Connecticut, and Massachusetts.

Devlin knew about the value of stolen artwork through his association with another gangster, Robert Wilson, who had at one point drafted Devlin's brother, also named Robert, to help him fence a Van Dyck masterpiece and twelve lesser-known paintings stolen in Providence in 1976 to a buyer in Tampa, Florida.

The buyer, however, turned out to be an undercover FBI agent, and Wilson, Robert Devlin, and a third associate were arrested, though ultimately only Wilson was convicted.

(Interestingly, the Van Dyck, which was by far the most valuable of the stolen artwork, disappeared as mysteriously as it appeared. There had been no testimony during the trial that reported from whom it had been stolen or how it had come into Wilson's possession. And four years after Wilson's conviction, the federal judge who sent him to prison approved a motion to return the Van Dyck painting to Wilson because prosecutors had never established that the painting had been stolen. Daniel Grieco, Wilson's lawyer, said he doesn't recall having gotten the painting back from the FBI.)

Devlin's other brother, Frank, scoffed at the possibility that Richard Devlin might have been involved in the Gardner theft, though. "It seems a little above him after all the heinous stuff he was alleged to have done in his life," he said. Frank Devlin was recently informed that his mobster brother had left what looked to be a diary in a bank's safety deposit box before his death. It had taken a decade to be turned over to the state.

"I might just have to open that diary up to see if there's any secrets about the Gardner heist or anything else in it," Frank said with a chuckle, still clearly not believing his brutal brother had any involvement.

Devlin remained his dangerous self to the end. In fact, he was wearing a bulletproof vest when he sat in a car with Stevie Rossetti and Richard Gillis, another mob associate, watching a social club on Bennington Street in East Boston, one day in March 1994. The club was operated by forces that had once been loyal to Ferrara and Russo. At 9:30 P.M. gunfire erupted at the three Salemme associates. When police arrived, they found Richard Devlin slumped behind the wheel of his 1994 Buick Skylark. He'd been shot in the head and was in critical condition; he died a few days later. Gillis suffered a bullet wound to the face in the encounter, but Rossetti escaped uninjured.

With Rossetti locked away and Devlin gone, Louis Royce's original confidants now seem improbable sources of good information on the Gardner theft. At their 2013 press conference, they called to the public for more tips. If they have a reason for choosing not to investigate Bobby Donati's old apartment for clues, they aren't saying what it is.

AFTERWORD

I'D BEEN FOLLOWING THE TRAIL of the Gardner masterpieces, stolen that dreary March night in 1990, for almost twenty years the day I found myself in Robert Gentile's living room, in the suburbs of Hartford, Connecticut. As I sat there across from him, it seemed at one key moment that the whole Gardner mystery might unfold before me.

Gentile, well into his seventies, still wore the leg bracelets that monitored his home confinement while he was on parole from his conviction for selling prescription painkillers to an undercover federal informant. He and I talked at length about how the FBI came to consider him the key figure in the abiding mystery of the Gardner masterpieces.

All the while, over a couple of pizzas I'd brought along from Regina's, his favorite pizza parlor in Boston, we were sizing each other up—me pressing him on the holes in his denials, and him seeing how much I knew and, I thought, trying to determine whether I could be trusted to be told something different.

Gentile has the look of someone who has worked with his hands: He spent much of his life laying pavement. His clothes, though old and worn, were by no means tattered. His face was fleshy and looked as though it belonged to a man far bigger than his five feet six inches and more than two hundred–pound frame. But Gentile's eyes were large and expressive, especially when we talked about things he was eager to discuss, such as the unfairness of the FBI in believing Elene Guarente, when she told a federal grand jury that she knew her husband, dying from cancer, had given at least one of the stolen masterpieces to Gentile.

But why, I pressed him, had he agreed to assist the FBI in its recovery efforts if ultimately he had no real access to the paintings? That need for an honest answer seemed to get through to him as we wrapped up our first session, and he walked me slowly, with the help of a wooden cane, to his front door. The late afternoon sun was peeking through the living room's heavy drapes and he stopped and asked me, for the first time that afternoon, to shut off the tape recorder I still was holding in my hand.

What, he wanted to know, was he going to get out of the book I was planning to write? I sensed he was asking me a different question, though: What would happen if he decided to tell a different story? I told him I would be prepared to work with him, but it would have to be something different from the denials he and his lawyer had been giving in court and to the media. "If we're going to work together, you've got to be open with me about everything: how you got involved and what happened to those paintings," I told him.

I could feel myself holding my breath. For about thirty seconds, Gentile thought about what I had said, his head held low. When he looked up, his eyes had gone dead, and it was obvious that the moment of reflection had passed.

"They [the feds] set me up and ruined my life," he said flatly.

I left Gentile frustrated but with a better understanding of his three-year involvement in the Gardner case and why the FBI was so convinced he could lead them to one or more of the masterpieces. Replaying the moment in my mind, I thought about why he hadn't taken the bait. There was money—potentially millions of dollars—to be had if he could facilitate the return of the paintings. And while I hadn't explicitly offered him a more immediate reward for his information, we both knew I was willing to try. So why not open up? Two reasons eventually occurred to me. He didn't want to be humiliated, and he was afraid for himself and his family.

If he did have possession of any of the stolen masterpieces but they had been destroyed in a hiding place he had made for them—in the ditch beneath the false-bottomed floor of his backyard shed—and he told the tale, he would face a lifetime of embarrassment for allowing the multimillion-dollar artwork to be ruined. Even with a $5 million reward on the table, this was no small thing to a man like Gentile. But perhaps more important, Gentile and his family would be vulnerable to whatever criminal gangs he may owe allegiance to.

I knew his family was paramount in Gentile's mind. During our talks, he constantly talked about his wife's ill health, and he aimed his utmost anger at the federal officials who had refused to release him from prison to visit his daughter before she died in 2013.

Before long it occurred to me that there was one person who might be able to get Gentile to open up: Vincent Ferrara, the former Boston mob leader I had been speaking to for several months through a shared acquaintance. I had reached out to Ferrara not long before I'd met with Gentile, in the hope of learning more about the battle for control of the Boston underworld after the death of Raymond Patriarca and the takedown of the Angiulo family in the mid-1980s. What I'd gotten, passed through our intermediary, was far more than I had expected: a detailed account of the underworld dealings between Ferrara's gang and "Cadillac Frank" Salemme's crew, as well as the confession made to Ferrara by Robert Donati, his driver and close friend, that Donati had pulled off the Gardner Museum theft.

With or without Gentile, the pieces were starting to fit. Donati's confession had a ring of truth, not only because of the enormous detail involved, but because it also, finally, included a motive for the Gardner heist: Donati intended to exchange whatever masterpieces were stolen for Ferrara's release from prison, because Ferrara was the only person who could protect Donati in the then-raging war between the Ferrara and Salemme gangs.

But Donati never got his wish. With the heat more intense than he'd ever imagined after stealing the paintings, Donati hid the art, perhaps in the hands of his friend Bobby Guarente, hoping that one day he could still gain his friend's release. Instead he suffered a brutal death.

Now, with the $5 million reward in front of Ferrara—something he wanted to share with Donati's family—I could see a way that the return of the masterpieces might be brokered.

Although Ferrara had been living a quiet, law-abiding life since release from prison in 2005, he might be willing to meet and talk with Gentile, and provide him assurance that no harm would come to him or his family if he gave the authorities what they were looking for, namely the location of the masterpieces, even if they were now ruined.

I contacted the intermediary, who got back to me almost immediately. He was willing to put the request to Ferrara and ask him if he would meet with Gentile, but he envisioned a problem none of us could solve.

As a recently released federal prisoner, Gentile had to abide by certain rules. One of them prevented him from meeting with anyone who had been convicted of a federal offense. Only a federal judge, acting on the request of the FBI or another US law enforcement agency, could release Gentile from that restriction. Despite what felt like the biggest break in the

Gardner case yet, arranging a meeting between Ferrara and Gentile was not something I could accomplish. But it also felt like just the sort of meeting the authorities, especially those involved who have labored so tirelessly over the case, would want to see happen, if not encourage.

But it was up to the feds to arrange such a meeting. I had taken the matter as far as I could or should as a reporter.

Just like the Boston police, and many others who'd tried to help over the years, ultimately I had to cede jurisdiction to the FBI. Thus far, they had been unwilling to act on my information. I had to stop there.

But while rebuffing my approach, the feds were trying their own initiative to force Gentile's cooperation, convinced that he continued to hold the keys to solving the Gardner mystery. On multiple occasions after his release from federal prison in January 2014, the FBI sent an undercover informant in to meet with Gentile at his home to convince him to engage in criminal activity. Saying he needed the money, Gentile was only too willing to discuss the scheme, to sell marijuana to high-rollers attending rock concerts at the XL Center in Hartford. And in one of their conversations, Gentile told the undercover informant just what the investigators wanted to hear to convince themselves that despite all his denials that Gentile did have access to the stolen Gardner paintings.

According to assistant US attorney Durham, Gentile told the informant that if the marijuana deal worked out he might be willing to sell him two of the stolen masterpieces for a half a million dollars. But, Durham was asked, why would Gentile be willing to sell the masterpieces for so much less than the $5 million that the Gardner Museum was offering for the artwork? At a 2015 bail hearing following Gentile's arrest for parole violations and selling a loaded weapon to the undercover informant, who was a convicted felon, Durham said that Gentile didn't trust the reward offer from the museum and federal investigators, and, even if he gained the $5 million reward, thought they would pursue and arrest him on trumped-up charges.

McGuigan, Gentile's lawyer, had another explanation. Gentile's claim was just another futile attempt to try to con someone into believing that he has access to the stolen paintings. "Everyone thinks [Gentile] knows where the Holy Grail is," McGuigan told the federal judge in a failed attempt to get Gentile released on bail. "I don't think he does."

Gentile has now turned seventy-nine and knows he will die in prison if he is found guilty of selling a weapon to a convicted felon, a charge which carries a ten-year sentence. As the investigators see it, his only recourse for release would then be to return the stolen Gardner paintings. But according to those who have visited him in jail, Gentile continues to insist that's no real option for him at all—he has no idea where the paintings are located.

AFTER TWENTY-FIVE YEARS, the biggest art theft in world history is still an open case. Despite the efforts of the Federal Bureau of Investigation, no one has been arrested and nothing has been recovered. In fact, there hasn't even been a single confirmed sighting of any of the thirteen stolen pieces. It is a disgrace that wouldn't be tolerated in European countries, where art is revered as a national treasure rather than collected by hedge fund managers and titans of industry.

How could two men disguised as police officers, but wearing what were obviously fake mustaches and private security uniforms that could have been bought at any army supply store, have pulled off such an extraordinary score? How could they have run roughshod through the museum's hallowed galleries, like hoodlums on an angry rampage, smashing glass facings from frames, cutting Rembrandts from their mountings, yet leave a Napoleonic banner unharmed after a long, futile effort to unscrew it from its encasement? And how could a museum, containing gallery after gallery of masterpieces and priceless antiques, allow itself to remain vulnerable to such a theft after being warned in no uncertain terms that members of one of Boston's toughest gangs were plotting to rob it?

Enter a vulnerable museum in dime-store disguises, take the first things that look expensive, and walk out the employee entrance. In the end it was a simple plan, and it didn't take a master to execute it. All it took was a motive and a few friends in low places, just the kind of job that Bobby Donati was perfect for.

But the crime remains unsolved, and the artwork missing. Perhaps if traditional investigative work could not provide the key to a recovery, maybe a nontraditional approach could be successful. Even if Richard DesLauriers' 2013 press conference had left something to be desired in the way of convincing details of how the theft had taken place and where the paintings had been hidden, the FBI Boston chief said at least one thing I agreed with: What was needed in any renewed efforts to locate the missing masterpieces was, quite simply, more people looking.

Although the FBI and the Gardner Museum had spent millions trying to locate the artwork via traditional investigative work, what had been missing from the approach was the public's commitment to the effort. A "crowdsourcing" campaign could garner public awareness and commitment toward playing a role in recovering the art. There needed to be an effort to show the people of Boston, if not art lovers everywhere, that what was stolen in that March 1990 heist was as much our loss as it was the museum's.

Anne Hawley had issued eloquent statements about that loss on several occasions in the past, but they seemed to have been forgotten in just a few days' time. Richard DesLauriers had made his plea for the public's help in 2013, but in the aftermath of the Boston Marathon bombing, which took place a month after his Gardner press conference, it had been all but forgotten.

It did bring in a number of leads—which were dutifully investigated without success—before the public seemingly moved on. But still others are out there who have been looking.

One is a man named Howard Winter. Winter, a longtime Boston gangster in his eighties, and James Melvin, who turned seventy a few years ago, had a novel idea. Rather than try to take the glory for themselves, as William Youngworth and others seem to have tried, Winter and Melvin chose to seek information from their friends in the underworld about the stolen artwork, sharing the opportunity in the hope of achieving results.

Winter and Melvin insisted that what they were *not* offering to do was to go undercover for the authorities—they were not about to flip on any former associates.

Instead, they pledged to do their own detective work among their past associates—and new ones to whom they were directed—and make known this specific message: The paintings had been missing for far too long. Whatever the reason they had been stolen—to ransom someone out of jail, for a fire sale to an interested customer, for bartering a trade for illicit contraband like drugs, weapons, or stolen diamonds—it had long been satisfied. They needed to be back on the museum's gallery walls now and the deal being offered—the $5 million reward by the museum and no prosecution for possession of stolen property—was more than adequate.

The two worked diligently on the assignment for several years. Melvin flew to Canada, Florida, and California to meet with those he thought knew something or could help. Their work was interrupted, however, by another venture the pair got involved with: an attempt by both men to help a lawyer they knew avoid making high-interest payments on $100,000 he had borrowed from two businessmen. The statements Melvin and Winter made to the two businessmen were considered extortion threats. Both men were indicted, pleaded guilty to the charges, and were put on probation in 2013. Winter was eighty-three at the time, and Melvin seventy.

But Melvin was diagnosed with a serious illness during this period, halting their efforts on behalf of the Gardner. In a recent interview, Winter said that Melvin's death, which came in early 2014, had robbed him of both his friend and his hopes his partner could help recover the stolen paintings. "Jimmy knew everyone, and there was no door that didn't open for him," Winter said. "I thought we were making progress, good progress, but I guess it wasn't meant to be."

Even if Winter's story does not have a happy ending, he is one more example of a shift in will for gaining the paintings' recovery. Because of the FBI's insistence that it is not interested in prosecuting those who might have possession of the artwork, the bad guys have joined the recovery effort. The agency has been successful in drawing out people like Howie Winter, Robert Gentile, Louis Royce, and others who believe the masterpieces belong back on the museum's walls for all of the public's enjoyment.

For now, though, Boston—and the rest of the art-loving world—is entering a second quarter-century without the Gardner masterpieces. The magic and the wonder that had captured the imagination of Louis Royce so keenly that he wanted to find a way to steal them has now turned—he like so many other notorious bad guys believes the paintings need to be returned to those galleries' walls.

A reminder of what their loss means to the city came to me recently as I stood on the steps of the Boston Public Library, which is located in the city center, Copley Square. The city's vibrancy can be felt here—as young and old rush in and out of the library—as can the city's history, with the square dating back to the 1800s and also the site of the two terrible terrorist bomb blasts that killed three people and injured hundreds at the 2013 Boston Marathon.

Isabella and John Gardner moved into the nearby Back Bay neighborhood soon after their marriage in 1860. It was there that they grew to be known as perhaps the city's most brilliant couple, entertaining the highest achievers in the arts and business. But their residence, and the two adjoining apartments they bought as well, proved to be too small to accommodate the artistic masterpieces the couple began purchasing on their frequent trips to Europe and the Orient.

Together they decided they would build a museum on a plot of land farther west of Copley Square, in the Fens neighborhood, and Mrs. Gardner moved quickly to realize that goal after her husband's sudden death from a stroke in 1898.

Hoping the museum would encourage a particularly American style of art as well as heighten the appreciation of the arts among all Bostonians, the building was the largest privately owned museum in the country when it opened to the public in 1903, until the Barnes Museum opened in Philadelphia in the 1920s and later the Getty in Los Angeles in the 1970s.

But the Gardner collection remains one of the nation's greatest treasures. Back in Copley Square, at the entrance of the Boston Public Library, two large statues welcome visitors to the library's original entrance. One is dedicated to scientific endeavor, the other to the arts.

On the pedestal that holds the elegant female form that majestically represents artistic achievement through the ages, eight names are inscribed: Phidias, Praxiteles, Michelangelo, Donatello, Raphael, Titian, Velasquez, and ... Rembrandt. The works of six of those masters are on public display at the Gardner Museum, and it is one of the few places in the world where so many of such masterpieces are so accessible. Yet today the Gardner is perhaps even better known for the thirteen pieces that are missing, including three Rembrandts.

My hope is that this this book will hasten their return.

ACKNOWLEDGMENTS

Ernest Hemingway's quote that working for a newspaper can help you be a better writer—"as long as you quit in time"—stuck in my mind over the past year as I researched and wrote *Master Thieves*. How was I going to make this book on the historic theft from the Isabella Stewart Gardner Museum more than the sum of my coverage for the *Boston Globe* if I had spent my entire career as a newspaperman?

If I have succeeded, recognition needs to be shared with the following people: Jack Driscoll, Matthew Storin, Martin Baron, and Brian McGrory, the *Globe* editors since the theft, who have afforded my interest in the case. Project editors Ben Bradlee Jr. and Mark Morrow have edited my longer pieces into the *Globe*. Colleagues with whom I have worked on individual articles since I began covering the story in 1997 include Ric Kahn, Judy Rakowsky, Sean Murphy, Joe Williams, Dan Golden, Larry Tye, Shelley Murphy, Patricia Nealon, Milton Valencia, and Scott Allen. Globe colleagues and friends with whom I have thought through how best to report and tell the story included Gerard M. O'Neill, Tom Farragher, Linda Matchan, Walter V. Robinson, Kevin Cullen, Jenna Russell, Matt Brelis, Charles Mansbach, Marcella Bombardieri, and Charles Kenney.

For me, none of it works unless the facts have been thoroughly researched and properly linked. *Globe* librarian Lisa Tuite and her able staff of deputies helped me connect the dots no matter how dim or distant they seemed to be. Special thanks to Marc Shechtman for assembling the discouragingly long list of art thefts in Massachusetts in recent years. The book *Crowdsourcing: Why the Power of the Crowd Is Driving the Future of Business* by Jeff Howe, an assistant professor at Northeastern University's Journalism Department, provided valuable insight as to how digital media could make the public collectively more aware of the loss of these masterpieces and effect a recovery.

Lynn Johnston, my literary agent, proved extraordinary both in marketing the proposal as well as helping to assemble the chapters into a narrative. Jeff Slate served an invaluable role assisting in turning a compelling collection of facts into a continuous story line. Benjamin Adams, my editor at PublicAffairs, had the original idea that if the secret to the theft lay within the Boston mob then we'd have a terrific book. I can attest that beyond being a good amateur detective he's also a worthy editor. Thanks to *Globe* colleague Alex Beam for putting us together.

Although I have maintained an arm's-length relationship with the FBI and federal prosecutors throughout, I have had high respect for the work by the agents in charge of the investigation over the years—Daniel J. Falzon, the late Neil Cronin, and since 2004, Geoff Kelly. The three have maintained their vigor and professionalism chasing after every lead brought to them, from going through diplomatic channels to view a print that hung on the wall of a businessman's house in Tokyo to touring warehouses in the South End with a psychic. That none of the stolen artwork has been recovered is no reflection on their professionalism and zeal. But they work for an agency that is foremost fiercely protective of its pride and privileges in the law enforcement community, and I maintain their performance, at least at the outset of the investigation, would have been enhanced by shared decision-making with state and local police departments. Special agent Joseph Butchka provided me with valuable perspective on Louis Royce's criminal exploits. Special agent David Nadolski provided valuable perspective on Carmello Merlino's criminal enterprise. Robert Wittman, former FBI special agent and member of its art theft squad, described how entwined the paths for recoveries can be.

I specialized in political and government corruption at the *Globe*, so I had much to learn about the background of the Boston organized crime scene, and for that I express my appreciation to former US attorneys Donald K. Stern and Michael J. Sullivan; former assistant US attorneys Brian Kelly, Brien T. O'Conner, and James J. McGovern; and members of the Massachusetts state police force, including Captain Joseph "Buddy" Saccardo, Lieutenant Thomas McLaughlin, Colonel Thomas J. Foley, and William "Beeper" McGreal. Boston police officers who spoke to me about their involvement in the original investigation or the city's crime scene included detectives Dan Rice, sergeant detective Robin DeMarco, Carl Washington, Martin Coleman, sergeant detective Joseph F. Fiandaca, and police commissioners Kathleen O'Toole and Edward Davis.

Other members of law enforcement that provided valuable expertise included Revere police captain William Gannon; Chelsea police chief Linda (Washburn) McCaul of the state Department of Correction fugitive squad and Diane Wiffin, press spokesperson; Weymouth police captain John Concannon; and Braintree detective David Jordan and now-retired chief Paul Frasier.

At the Gardner, Anne Hawley, its director since six months before the theft, has sought to rebuild the museum with a vision that Mrs. Gardner would have appreciated, turning it into a gleaming, modern-day cultural landmark with its masterpieces serving as a beacon for artistic endeavor, and not just the site of the world's largest art theft. I accept that her decision to decline my request for assistance in this book was motivated by her interest in concentrating on the museum's future, not its past, and not any differences with my past reporting. Museum communications specialist Catharine Burton Deely was a delight to work with.

Museum board members Arnold S. Hiatt (now emeritus trustee) and Francis W. Hatch Jr. (who passed away in 2010) as well as deputy director Linda Hewitt provided me with an understanding of the museum's decision-making process, including its frustrations in embarking on a major fund-raising campaign in the 1980s.

Other museum employees, especially those familiar with its security operations, have been generous with their time and recollections, including security directors Lyle Grindle and deputy director Lawrence P. O'Brien; Tom Johnson and Jon-Paul Kroger, who trained incoming guards and night watchmen; and Steven R. Keller, whose firm was hired to review the museum's security needs before the theft.

I was given valuable advice about art theft and recovery in general and specific cases from international police and private detectives, such as Julian Radcliffe of the Art Loss Registry; Christopher Marinello of Art Recovery International; Richard Ellis of the Art Management Group; Charles Hill, former detective for Scotland Yard; and the late Charles Moore. Boston attorney George Abrams, both a collector and a legal specialist in art theft cases, recalled in fascinating detail several cases from decades ago in Boston and Cambridge that drew attention.

My family and friends kept me upbeat and focused during the long process of putting pen to paper. Friends first—Edwin and Imelda Cosme, Arnold Cohen, Annie Crane, Rosellen Cappucci, Lynda Burchfield, Kate Sullivan, Marc Mamigonian, Arpie Davis, Joshua Resnick, and Joan Sprout Tarbox. And though the size of my extended family could make up a decent day-game crowd at Fenway Park, those around me in Section 30, Row 6, would be my sisters Karolyn Kurkjian-Jones and Elizabeth Kurkjian-Henry and her husband, John; daughter Erica and her husband, Sean Parrell; son Adam and his wife, Amy Ruggere-Kurkjian; and my three cherub grandchildren, Theodore, Jillian, and Emily Parrell.

RESOURCES

CHAPTER ONE

I interviewed Louis F. Royce dozens of time both in prison and out after our first meeting at a minimum security facility in 2007, and I was able to confirm almost all of what he told me through official records, including FBI files, court documents, and hospital records he provided, as well as newspaper articles and interviews with others. Two former criminal associates confirmed his association with the Rossetti gang in East Boston. The February 1981 robbery of the Newton home, in which he, Stephen Rossetti, and Ralph Rossetti stole numbered prints by Dalí and Chagall, is described in Middlesex County Superior Court documents, Newton police files, and the *Newton Tab* newspaper. Royce's description of the robbery of the Rockland Trust branch in Hanover was confirmed by bank officials, *Quincy Patriot Ledger* articles, and police interviews. Timesheets kept by the Massachusetts Department of Correction confirmed that Richard Devlin had been released on furlough from a nearby forestry camp in sufficient time to have participated in the actual bank robbery. Royce's account of spending nights as a runaway boy inside the museum could be confirmed only by his showing me the hideaways inside the museum where he says he slept. His account of using a lift to determine whether the museum's second-floor window was unlocked was corroborated by a Devlin family member. The account that FBI special agent Edward Clark gave to Gardner officials of the scheme Royce and Rossetti had to rob the Gardner in 1981 was confirmed through museum officials and handwritten notes kept by the museum of its meeting with Clark.

CHAPTER TWO

Interviews with Lyle Grindle, retired chief of security for the Gardner Museum, and William P. McAuliffe, former head of security at the Museum of Fine Arts, provided the information about their walk-through of the Gardner on the eve of the heist. McAuliffe, as well as several MFA security personnel who were working there at the time, helped me understand what had happened when two men dressed as Boston police officers sought entry into the MFA after midnight following the Martin Luther King celebration in January 1990. Those personnel also provided information on the February 1989 theft of a Yuan vase, valued at $1 million, from the MFA, as did coverage of the arrest of the thieves in the *New York Times*. Information on the Gardner's financial woes during the 1980s and board of trustees' inability to agree on an ambitious fund-raising plan to deal with growing problems with the museum's security and building environment issues were gained from interviews with some board members, the museum's annual reports submitted to the Suffolk County Probate Court, and a twenty-page report written in 1989 by director Roland "Bump" Hadley summarizing his frustrations in dealing with the trustees. The account of the robbers dressed as police officers waiting in a "hatchback" before the heist is drawn from interviews with three young people who saw them in the car after the three had left a party in a nearby apartment building and began goofing off for a few minutes on Palace Road. The description of the actual theft is drawn from several long interviews with Richard "Rick" Abath, the night watchman who made the fateful decision to allow the thieves into the museum; Boston police official reports on the break-in; and interviews with the officers who responded to the robbery. The museum provided me access to its own files on the break-in including the transcript of the motion-detector equipment, which provided a second-by-second account of the robbers' eighty-eight minutes inside the museum.

CHAPTER THREE

After competing with me for decades on the Gardner heist story, Tom Mashberg, lead reporter on the crime for the *Boston Herald*, agreed to be interviewed about his 1997 bombshell story that he had had a clandestine viewing of the stolen Rembrandt seascape, *Storm on the Sea of Galilee*. Our interview was conditioned on the pledge that Mashberg would be able to read and approve what I wrote of it in my book, and if we couldn't come to an agreement, we would let a mutual friend decide. We never had to seek our friend's intercession as Tom's edits were few and made solely for accuracy's sake. The confidential note that Youngworth wrote to Mashberg alluding to the backstory on how the viewing had taken place was provided by a source but was confirmed by Mashberg. Youngworth's ties to the Rossetti gang and the assassination of his best friend in his presence are described in a 1982 affidavit given by Massachusetts state police sergeant Thomas McLaughlin and filed in Suffolk County Superior Court. Prosecutors from the office of US attorney Donald Stern were interviewed on their dealings with Mashberg and Youngworth for background.

CHAPTER FOUR

The museum provided me with the letters Anne Hawley received from an anonymous source, and their wording and response to them was confirmed by FBI officials. *Globe* editors described their decision-making on why the paper agreed to insert a numeral in the exchange rate table that ran in the *Globe* on May 1, 1994. The efforts in 1999 to get Pope John Paul to issue an appeal on behalf of the stolen paintings was revealed in a report prepared by Investigative Group International, the Washington, DC-based investigative firm the museum retained to help in the probe. I was introduced to Jurek Rokoszynski when the museum hired him in 2005 and followed his tracking of the one tip he was assigned to investigate to its futile end, and interviewed the ex-convict who had provided it and the former Boston art collector whom it wrongly focused on more than a year later. In interviews former Massachusetts governor Michael S. Dukakis, former Boston mayor Raymond Flynn, and retired state police head Thomas Foley spoke of their frustrations with the FBI having assumed total control of the investigation rather than drawing on the assistance of the Boston and Massachusetts state police. The office of US Senator John F. Kerry shared with me its communications with FBI director Robert S. Mueller on seeking more resources for the investigation. The FBI spokesman at DC headquarters declined comment. Robert K. Wittman, undercover agent for the FBI's art theft squad, wrote of his experiences on the Gardner case in his book *Priceless: How I Went Undercover to Rescue the World's Stolen Treasures.*

CHAPTER FIVE

For more coverage of the recovery of the Cezanne stolen from the home of Herbert Bakwin, see "What a Steal" in the December 17, 2000, edition of the *Boston Globe Sunday Magazine.* For the recovery of the other paintings stolen from Bakwin's home, see "1978 Art Heist Solved" in the *Boston Globe,* February 1, 2006.

CHAPTER SIX

I interviewed Robert Gentile for more than five hours over three days in January 2014, only a few days after his release from federal prison for selling prescription drugs to an undercover federal informant. Gentile also gave me permission to view the legal files maintained on his case by his criminal defense lawyer, A. Ryan McGuigan of Hartford. Gentile also provided me with access to the shed in his backyard that federal agents scoured through, believing he had kept the stolen Gardner paintings inside a large plastic container in the ditch beneath the shed's false floor. Edmund Mahony's coverage of Gentile's prosecution in the *Hartford Courant* was fair and complete, and his May 19, 2013, profile of Gentile provided valuable background. The cocaine ring Robert F. Guarente and Robert Luisi Jr. operated in the late 1990s is described in detail in a thirty-one-page affidavit filed by DEA agent Steven C. Story in the federal cocaine distributing case brought against Guarente in US District Court in Boston. For coverage of the brutal shooting death of Luisi's father, half-brother, and cousin while having lunch in a Charlestown restaurant on November 6, 1995, see coverage in the *Boston Globe* and the *Boston Herald*.

CHAPTER SEVEN

Florian "Al" Monday told me in an interview how he had approached Gentile to connect with Robert Guarente in Maine in hopes that Guarente would be able to secure photographs of the stolen Gardner paintings. In that interview, Monday acknowledged it was he who had made out the list, tucked inside the *Boston Herald*'s front-page coverage of the theft and recovered by FBI agents in Gentile's basement, that estimated what the thirteen stolen pieces might bring on the black market. Elene Guarente spoke to me several times by phone about her belief that her late husband, Robert, had possession of some of the Gardner paintings and had turned over one or more of them to his longtime friend Robert Gentile in the parking lot of a Portland restaurant in the early 2000s. Earle E. Berghman spoke to me about his belief that Guarente, his longtime friend, did have possession of the stolen paintings and his efforts to consummate a recovery effort, through Boston attorney Bernard Grossberg, with Guarente's daughter. A Maine state police document, dated May 3, 1991, said Berghman, Guarente, Francis Strazzula, and William J. Norton were under investigation for possible links to armored car robberies, drug trafficking, and the death of an associate, James Marks.

CHAPTER EIGHT

The profile of David Turner was drawn from multiple sources including files maintained by Braintree and Tewksbury police, Massachusetts state police, and court records. Turner was mentioned frequently in reports conducted by state police investigating cocaine trafficking out of the TRC auto radiator garage in Dorchester in the early 1990s as he was in the federal prosecution of a scheme to rob the Loomis-Fargo armored car headquarters in Easton, Massachusetts. Chris Ruggiero, his boyhood friend, spoke to me about his belief that Turner was about to pen a tell-all book about his life in crime and possible involvement in the Gardner heist. However, Turner repeatedly denied those intentions in an email exchange with me in June 2013 from Otisville Federal Penitentiary in New York. He has since been transferred closer to his Massachusetts home and is now incarcerated in a federal prison in Danbury, Connecticut. George Pappas's decision to flip on Turner is detailed in the investigative files of state police trooper Edward Whelan. Pappas's assassination a few days before he was to testify against Turner is detailed in Braintree police records and interviews with Braintree police chief Paul Frasier. I interviewed several members of the late George Reissfelder's family and his longtime friend Robert Beauchamp, now in custody in Bay State Correctional Center in Massachusetts, about Reissfelder's possible involvement in the Gardner theft and his ties to the criminal gang centered at Carmello Merlino's Dorchester garage. The fourteen-month period between 1998 and 1999 in which Merlino sought to orchestrate the return of the Gardner artwork while he schemed to rob the Loomis Fargo headquarters is detailed in the federal indictment against Merlino, Turner, Stephen Rossetti, and Merlino's nephew William for the robbery attempt. Also, I drew on a 225-page unpublished diary written by Anthony Romano, the FBI's undercover informant inside Merlino's operation, to detail the twin schemes taking place inside Merlino's garage.

CHAPTER NINE

Former US attorney Donald Stern was interviewed in 2013, William P. Youngworth in 2003, Louis Royce between 2007 and 2014, and retired FBI agents Robert Wittman and David Nadolski in 2014. I covered for the *Globe* several of the criminal court sessions against Robert Gentile at US District Court in Hartford, including his pleading guilty to selling prescription drugs to an undercover informant and his sentencing.

CHAPTER TEN

The *Boston Globe* and *Boston Herald* provided extensive coverage of the war between the two rival gangs, one headed by Frank Salemme and the other by Vincent Ferrara, Robert Carrozza, and J. R. Russo, to assume control of the Boston underworld following the indictment of Gennaro Angiulo and his brothers in 1985. *The New England Mafia: Illustrated* by Kevin Johnston also provided background. Valuable information on the war between the gangs was also contained in the US criminal indictment in Worcester, Massachusetts, in 1997 against fifteen members of the Boston underworld.

CHAPTER ELEVEN

The Underboss: The Rise and Fall of a Mafia Family by Dick Lehr and Gerard M. O'Neill provided the best background of the Angiulo family's control of the Boston underworld. Alerted by Boston attorney Francis J. DiMento that Vincent Ferrara was trying to unravel the Gardner case, I spoke on more than a dozen occasions with an intermediary on Ferrara's behalf about Ferrara's discussions with his late driver, Robert Donati, about the crime. I also interviewed two Donati family members about Donati's possible involvement. Donati's FBI files, obtained through a Freedom of Information Act request, also provided useful background on his life in crime. A search of the book by legendary art thief Myles Connor, *The Art of the Heist: Confessions of a Master Thief,* also provided background on

Donati and his alleged involvement in a prior art theft. The account of Donati at The Shack was provided by a Donati friend from Revere who was visiting the hangout at the time. Ferrara's background in the mob is described in the 1990 federal indictment to which he decided to plead guilty two years later, and US justice Mark Wolf's decision to free Ferrara because the prosecution had withheld exculpatory evidence from his lawyers was the final document in the criminal case file.

AFTERWORD

Longtime Boston gang leader Howard Winter provided me with the details of his efforts to recover the paintings in two brief telephone interviews. Mrs. Gardner's life deserves a fuller treatment than I provided here but I learned enough about her commitment to the arts and her zeal to share that love with Bostonians and Americans everywhere from *Mrs. Jack: A Biography of Isabella Stewart Gardner* by Louise Hall Tharp; *The Art of Scandal: The Life and Times of Isabella Stewart Gardner* by Douglass Shand-Tucci; *The Isabella Stewart Gardner Museum: A Companion Guide and History* by Hilliard T. Goldfarb; and *Boston Globe* historical files.

INDEX

Boston Globe

STEPHEN KURKJIAN is one of the most acclaimed investigative reporters in the country. A forty-year veteran of the *Boston Globe*, he is the paper's former Washington bureau chief and a founding member of its investigative Spotlight Team. Kurkjian has won more than twenty-five national and regional awards including the Pulitzer Prize on three occasions. He is a graduate of Boston University and Suffolk Law School and lives in Boston.

PublicAffairs is a publishing house founded in 1997. It is a tribute to the standards, values, and flair of three persons who have served as mentors to countless reporters, writers, editors, and book people of all kinds, including me.

I. F. STONE, proprietor of *I. F. Stone's Weekly*, combined a commitment to the First Amendment with entrepreneurial zeal and reporting skill and became one of the great independent journalists in American history. At the age of eighty, Izzy published *The Trial of Socrates*, which was a national bestseller. He wrote the book after he taught himself ancient Greek.

BENJAMIN C. BRADLEE was for nearly thirty years the charismatic editorial leader of *The Washington Post*. It was Ben who gave the *Post* the range and courage to pursue such historic issues as Watergate. He supported his reporters with a tenacity that made them fearless and it is no accident that so many became authors of influential, best-selling books.

ROBERT L. BERNSTEIN, the chief executive of Random House for more than a quarter century, guided one of the nation's premier publishing houses. Bob was personally responsible for many books of political dissent and argument that challenged tyranny around the globe. He is also the founder and longtime chair of Human Rights Watch, one of the most respected human rights organizations in the world.

.　　.　　.

For fifty years, the banner of Public Affairs Press was carried by its owner Morris B. Schnapper, who published Gandhi, Nasser, Toynbee, Truman, and about 1,500 other authors. In 1983, Schnapper was described by *The Washington Post* as "a redoubtable gadfly." His legacy will endure in the books to come.

Peter Osnos, *Founder and Editor-at-Large*